**Current**
**CONTROVERSIES**

# Medical Use of
# Illicit Drugs

# Other Books in the Current Controversies Series

# Medical Use of Illicit Drugs

Kathleen Cronin, Book Editor

GREENHAVEN
PUBLISHING

Published in 2020 by Greenhaven Publishing, LLC
353 3rd Avenue, Suite 255, New York, NY 10010

Copyright © 2020 by Greenhaven Publishing, LLC

First Edition

Articles in Greenhaven Publishing anthologies are often edited for length to meet page
requirements. In addition, original titles of these works are changed to clearly present
the main thesis and to explicitly indicate the author's opinion. Every effort is made to
ensure that Greenhaven Publishing accurately reflects the original intent of the authors.
Every effort has been made to trace the owners of the copyrighted material.

Cover image: The Washington Post/Getty Images

**Library of Congress Cataloging-in-Publication Data**

Names: Cronin, Kathleen, editor.
Title: Medical use of illicit drugs / Kathleen Cronin, book editor.
Description: First edition. | New York : Greenhaven Publishing, 2020. | Series: Current
controversies | Includes bibliographical references and index. | Audience: Grades 9–12.
Identifiers: LCCN 2019024929 | ISBN 9781534506114 (library
binding) | ISBN 9781534506107 (paperback)
Subjects: LCSH: Hallucinogenic drugs—Therapeutic use—United States. | Hallucinogenic
drugs—Research—United States. | Hallucinogenic drugs—Therapeutic use—Law and
legislation—United States. | Hallucinogenic drugs—Research—Law and legislation—
United States. | Marijuana—Therapeutic use—Law and legislation—United States.
Classification: LCC RM324.8 .M43 2020 | DDC 615.7/883—dc23
LC record available at https://lccn.loc.gov/2019024929

*Manufactured in the United States of America*

Website: http://greenhavenpublishing.com

# Contents

## Chapter 1: Does Medical Research with Illicit Drugs Benefit Patients?

*Monica Dybuncio and Ryan Jaslow*

Physicians, scientists, and neuropsychopharmacology researchers are uncovering remarkable and potentially game-changing treatments for chronic neurological symptoms. However, the drugs they are using are controlled substances with many potential negative health effects.

### Yes: Medical Research with Illicit Drugs Benefits Patients

*Phillip Francis*

Patients suffering from cancer, PTSD, depression, anxiety, and addiction are finding relief in clinical trials where doctors are treating these chronic conditions in new ways with illicit drugs.

*Denis Campbell*

Distinguished academics and institutions are investigating the potential therapeutic effects of psychotropic drugs for the first time in decades, and they are finding surprising results.

### No: Medical Research with Illicit Drugs Does Not Benefit Patients

*Veljko Dubljević*

In international treaties and drug control policies, standardized scheduling of substances determines how they are legally regulated. Many experts believe that those schedules have little or no footing in scientific evidence, as they lack a public health or pharmacological basis. Contemporary scientists aim to better quantify potential harm but maintain that the risks of some substances far outweigh the potential benefits.

*Jennifer Whitlock*

Thousands of Americans seek medical care outside of the US every year. They are motivated by a variety of factors, including treatment with illicit drugs, cost savings, insurance incentives, and bypassing rules and regulations. There are many factors to consider, as the quality of training and patient care can vary widely, creating potential risks for patients.

## Chapter 2: Is the Current Drug Approval and Regulation Process the Best Option for Patients?

*US Food and Drug Administration*

The Center for Drug Evaluation and Research (CDER) evaluates potential innovations in medical drug treatments in the United States. The center's evidence-based processes and requirements ensure that medical professionals are informed and patients are safe taking FDA-approved medications.

## Yes: Regulated, Research-Based Drug Approval Protocols Using Legal Substances Produce the Best Medical Treatments for Patients

*Monique Ellis*

In 2018, the FDA approved more than fifty new drugs, devices, and diagnostic tools to address a range of medical conditions. Approval efforts included remedies for rare diseases, more effective treatments for dangerous diseases, and new medicines to protect populations from potential biological warfare.

*Monique Ellis*

Technological, scientific, and medical innovators have teamed up to introduce remarkable new patient treatments this year: telemedicine, artificial organs, wireless brain sensors, and wearable health devices are just some of the exciting new therapies being made available.

## No: Regulated, Research-Based Drug Approval Protocols with Strictly Legal Substances Do Not Offer the Most Innovative Treatments

*Michael White*

George W. Bush defined a conflict between medical research and pro-life politics. His ban on research with embryonic stem cells created insurmountable obstacles to ongoing research. A 2008 order, "Removing Barriers to Responsible Scientific Research," opened the path for new analysis and research with these controversial cells. Discoveries made in the last decade are at the point of entirely eliminating the conflict surrounding the use of stem cells.

*Comment Central*

Our regulatory system of control over the drug approval process is expensive and inordinately difficult to navigate. Scientific and medical advances have improved the quality of life for patients everywhere. At the same time, regulations and government entities have created a confusing, slow development process with exploding costs that may not serve patients' needs.

*Dean Baker*

Patent monopolies have financed research and drug development in the US for decades. This approach adds enormous cost to American health care in the form of unlimited pricing opportunities afforded to the manufacturer of a patented drug. Government-funded research with private entities on long-term contracts would likely lower costs, increase transparency, improve partnerships, and advance innovation, but at present the drug approval process does not benefit patients.

# Chapter 3: Does Current Regulation of Illicit Drugs Inhibit Medical Innovation?

### Christopher-Paul Milne and Kenneth I. Kaitin

The landscape of global health becomes more complicated as fewer resources are devoted to ensuring public education and well-being. Rethinking our approach, adding regulatory flexibility, including now-illegal drugs in clinical and research trials, and incentivizing research and development in disease areas with high unmet needs will make a positive difference for patients.

## Yes: Current Regulations of Illicit Drugs Inhibit Scientific and Medical Research

### David Nutt

International attempts to eliminate recreational drug use have had economic, social, and human costs for countries across the globe. Those efforts have also created insurmountable barriers to the study, analysis, and creation of innovative medical therapies for patients suffering from a variety of medical conditions.

### David Trilling

Evidence exists that clarifies the medical value of cannabis to treat a variety of health issues. Legal changes in the status of the drug continue to outpace research findings clarifying how the plant and its derivatives impact human health. New questions arise regularly; a flexible approach to new research and development and more evidence-based analysis are required.

### David Nutt

For decades, regulations have been designed to limit access to drugs that are deemed dangerous to public health. Restrictions have impacted pharmacology and therapeutics research with disastrous results. Contemporary efforts to control new drugs in development censors information and creates real obstacles to scientific progress.

## No: Current Regulation of Illicit Drugs Does Not Inhibit Scientific and Medical Research

*Dr. C. M. Helm-Clark*

The term "medical marijuana" means different things to different people. Clarifying the details and the legal status of cannabis and its derivatives in the United States provides patients with more information and allows doctors and patients alike to make informed decisions on potential medical treatments available.

*Stevyn Colgan*

In many cases, the roots of drug use and abuse are physical or emotional pain and suffering. In their efforts to understand patients' conditions, scientists inadvertently caused drug addiction by researching and testing with unknown substances.

# Chapter 4: Should the Medical Use of Illicit Drugs Be Exempt from Legal Repercussions?

*Mark A. R. Kleiman, Jonathan P. Caulkins, Angela Hawken, and Beau Kilmer*

Current research efforts are paying little attention to some innovative policies with substantial potential to provide better health outcomes for patients. By concentrating on the biological, psychological, and sociological aspects of drug taking, scientists are limiting their ability to minimize the damage of drug abuse and missing the potential of research efforts with substances that may currently be illegal.

## Yes: Using Illicit Drugs for Medical Purposes Should Be Exempt from Legal Repercussions

*The Emplawyerologist Firm*

Marijuana possession and use is a federal crime in the United States in 2019. The federal government does not believe users of medical cannabis are protected from criminal prosecution. But twenty-eight states have legalized the medical use of marijuana, changing the scope of responsibility for leaders accountable for human resources.

## No: Using Illicit Drugs for Medical Purposes Should Not Be Exempt from Legal Repercussions

# Foreword

"Controversy" is a word that has an undeniably unpleasant connotation. It carries a definite negative charge. Controversy can spoil family gatherings, spread a chill around classroom and campus discussion, inflame public discourse, open raw civic wounds, and lead to the ouster of public officials. We often feel that controversy is almost akin to bad manners, a rude and shocking eruption of that which must not be spoken or thought of in polite, tightly guarded society. To avoid controversy, to quell controversy, is often seen as a public good, a victory for etiquette, perhaps even a moral or ethical imperative.

Yet the studious, deliberate avoidance of controversy is also a whitewashing, a denial, a death threat to democracy. It is a false sterilizing and sanitizing and superficial ordering of the messy, ragged, chaotic, at times ugly processes by which a healthy democracy identifies and confronts challenges, engages in passionate debate about appropriate approaches and solutions, and arrives at something like a consensus and a broadly accepted and supported way forward. Controversy is the megaphone, the speaker's corner, the public square through which the citizenry finds and uses its voice. Controversy is the life's blood of our democracy and absolutely essential to the vibrant health of our society.

Our present age is certainly no stranger to controversy. We are consumed by fierce debates about technology, privacy, political correctness, poverty, violence, crime and policing, guns, immigration, civil and human rights, terrorism, militarism, environmental protection, and gender and racial equality. Loudly competing voices are raised every day, shouting opposing opinions, putting forth competing agendas, and summoning starkly different visions of a utopian or dystopian future. Often these voices attempt to shout the others down; there is precious little listening and considering among the cacophonous din. Yet listening and considering, too, are essential to the health of a democracy. If controversy is democracy's lusty lifeblood, respectful listening and careful thought are its higher faculties, its brain, its conscience.

Current Controversies does not shy away from or attempt to hush the loudly competing voices. It seeks to provide readers with as wide and representative as possible a range of articulate voices on any given controversy of the day, separates each one out to allow it to be heard clearly and fairly, and encourages careful listening to each of these well-crafted, thoughtfully expressed opinions, supplied by some of today's leading academics, thinkers, analysts, politicians, policy makers, economists, activists, change agents, and advocates. Only after listening to a wide range of opinions on an issue, evaluating the strengths and weaknesses of each argument, assessing how well the facts and available evidence mesh with the stated opinions and conclusions, and thoughtfully and critically examining one's own beliefs and conscience can the reader begin to arrive at his or her own conclusions and articulate his or her own stance on the spotlighted controversy.

This process is facilitated and supported in each Current Controversies volume by an introduction and chapter overviews that provide readers with the essential context they need to begin engaging with the spotlighted controversies, with the debates surrounding them, and with their own perhaps shifting or nascent opinions on them. Chapters are organized around several key questions that are answered with diverse opinions representing all points on the political spectrum. In its content, organization, and methodology, readers are encouraged to determine the authors' point of view and purpose, interrogate and analyze the various arguments and their rhetoric and structure, evaluate the arguments' strengths and weaknesses, test their claims against available facts and evidence, judge the validity of the reasoning, and bring into clearer, sharper focus the reader's own beliefs and conclusions and how they may differ from or align with those in the collection or those of classmates.

Research has shown that reading comprehension skills improve dramatically when students are provided with compelling, intriguing, and relevant "discussable" texts. The subject matter of these collections could not be more compelling, intriguing, or urgently relevant to today's students and the world they are poised to inherit. The anthologized articles also provide the basis for stimulating, lively, and passionate classroom debates. Students who are compelled to anticipate objections to their own argument and identify the flaws in those of an opponent read more carefully, think more critically, and steep themselves in relevant context, facts, and information more thoroughly. In short, using discussable text of the kind provided by every single volume in the Current Controversies series encourages close reading, facilitates reading comprehension, fosters research, strengthens critical thinking, and greatly enlivens and energizes classroom discussion and participation. The entire learning process is deepened, extended, and strengthened.

If we are to foster a knowledgeable, responsible, active, and engaged citizenry, we must provide readers with the intellectual, interpretive, and critical-thinking tools and experience necessary to make sense of the world around them and of the all-important debates and arguments that inform it. We must encourage them not to run away from or attempt to quell controversy but to embrace it in a responsible, conscientious, and thoughtful way, to sharpen and strengthen their own informed opinions by listening to and critically analyzing those of others. This series encourages respectful engagement with and analysis of current controversies and competing opinions and fosters a resulting increase in the strength and rigor of one's own opinions and stances. As such, it helps readers assume their rightful place in the public square and provides them with the skills necessary to uphold their awesome responsibility—guaranteeing the continued and future health of a vital, vibrant, and free democracy.

# Introduction

> *"To raise new questions, and new possibilities, to regard old problems from a new angle, requires creative imagination and marks real advance in science."*
>
> —*Albert Einstein*

Human beings have been ingesting healing and psychotropic substances from the natural world in rituals, as balms, and as medicinal cures for all of recorded history. For the last hundred years, organized societies have worked to regulate the study, cultivation, manufacture, distribution, sale, and use of a variety of these substances with mixed results. Today, dramatically differing values, complex legal debates, cutting-edge scientific research, and evolving social and cultural dynamics all contribute to the environment of controversy surrounding the medical use of illicit drugs.

Medical and scientific invention has played a critical role in the development of illicit drug use across history. Therapeutic innovations developed to reduce human suffering and introduced during the American Civil War (1861–1865) and the early twentieth century were not extensively analyzed before they were put into use with the general population. At one time, amphetamines, cocaine, cannabis, and heroin were all uncontrolled substances. They were treated as legal, prescribed medications or over-the-counter treatments, available to all in the US. Over the decades, as authorities developed a greater understanding of the public health risks and potential negative behavioral impacts associated with the use of these drugs, the need for greater control surfaced.

International agreement and cooperative control of illicit drugs was initiated by the United States in 1909.[1] Fear and concern about opium and cocaine addiction—and its associated criminal activity, negative health effects, and the perceived lowered morality of addicts—brought representatives of thirteen nations together in Shanghai, China, at the International Opium Commission, which led to the signing of the International Opium Convention in 1912.[2] Between 1909 and 1940, there were additional treaties focused on drugs and their use and distribution adopted under the auspices of the League of Nations.[3] When the United Nations was established following World War II, it took over the enforcement of all existing international conventions and treaties.

The UN led an effort in 1960 to combine treaties focused on controlled substances into one set of standards. The Single Convention on Narcotic Drugs of 1961 consolidated multiple guidelines into a set of standard conventions covering opium, coca, and cannabis.[4] During the 1960s, illicit drug use increased as drugs became more widely available to the public in the midst of social movements driving legal and cultural change. During this time, the US military, the Central Intelligence Agency (CIA), and scientific and medical researchers studied amphetamines, LSD, and cocaine as potential tools without fully understanding the long-term human impact of exposure to these drugs. As availability and usage increased, black markets developed. But authorities in most jurisdictions did not have laws in place under which they could arrest or prosecute either users or distributors of illicit drugs.

The Convention on Psychotropic Substances of 1971 is a United Nations treaty that defined drugs according to their perceived risk and established rules aimed at the prohibition and criminalization of the use and distribution of substances, in addition to the restriction of imports and exports. The Convention requires member states to create laws in their countries to implement and execute the guidelines included in the convention.

Schedule 1 drugs are defined as those "claimed to create a serious risk to public health, whose potential therapeutic value is not currently acknowledged by the Commission on Narcotic Drugs." These include cannabis, LSD, and other psychedelics and amphetamine-type stimulants like MDMA (Ecstasy). Schedule 2 drugs are amphetamine-type substances with known therapeutic uses, including Delta-9 THC amphetamine and Methylphenidate (Ritalin). Schedule 3 substances are fast-acting barbiturates and strongly sedative products, which have known therapeutic applications and high risk for abuse. These include Flunitrazepam, Buprenorphine, and Cathine. Schedule 4 drugs are weaker barbiturates and substances identified with known therapeutic uses that still pose risk for dependence.[5]

The implementation of the 1971 Convention had worldwide consequences and inadvertently created onerous barriers to medical scientific research. Substances that had been available for research for decades—studied for their potential to cure and minimize the impacts of complex medical problems—were no longer available. The materials required for research quickly became restricted behind a complex legal bureaucracy despite their early promise in clinical trials.

Social change in the early 1970s drove new efforts to decriminalize substances. Beginning in 1973, states crafted new laws in response to voter initiatives, and over the next twenty years changing attitudes and understanding eroded uniform and steadfast opposition to many drugs as scientific innovation demonstrated new possibilities for a variety of illegal substances.

Scientists made consistent efforts in Western nations to build medical exemptions from the 1961 and '71 conventions. This, as well as developing independent perspectives, led to the legalization of medical cannabis in California in 1996. Since then, twenty-three additional states have legalized the medical use of cannabis, and twelve states have legalized recreational use of cannabis since 2012, when Colorado and Washington both implemented initiatives approved by wide margins of voters in those states.

Between 1991 and 2019, the crisis of the illicit use of opioid medications has escalated across the US.[6] Pharmaceutical organizations began active advocacy for opioid use in pain management in the early 1990s. Assured that there was a low incidence of addiction, a sharp increase in physician prescriptions led to a dramatic increase in the use of these drugs for pain management. A decade later, as the health risks associated with their use and the social costs of addiction became clear, public health efforts began in earnest to educate the public and reduce prescriptions of opioid medications. Opioid users have turned to heroin in the absence of the legally prescribed medications their doctor gave them for pain, compounding a complex social, political, and economic crisis surrounding the medical use of a controlled substance.

There are opposing viewpoints on the medical use of illicit drugs and differing perspectives on the creation of legal controls that limit availability, access, research, and use of these drugs. Scientists, politicians, commentators, and other experts argue these positions in *Current Controversies: Medical Use of Illicit Drugs*, shedding light on the many important perspectives worthy of consideration when trying to understand this complex and evolving issue.

## Notes

1. "The 1912 Hague International Opium Convention," United Nations Office on Drugs and Crime, New York, January 23, 2009.
2. "The History and Development of the Leading International Drug Control Conventions, prepared for the Canadian Senate Special Committee on Illegal Drugs," Jay Sinha, Law and Government Division, Library of Parliament, February 21, 2001, ttps://sencanada.ca/content/sen/committee/371/ille/library/history_3.htm.
3. "United Nations Convention on Psychotropic Substances," UN Office on Drugs and Crime, New York, February 21, 1971, www.unodc.org/PDF/convention_1971_en.pdf.
4. "The History and Development of the Leading International Drug Control Conventions, prepared for the Canadian Senate Special Committee on Illegal Drugs," by Jay Sinha, Law and Government Division, Library of Parliament,

February 21, 2001, https://sencanada.ca/content/sen/committee/371/ille/library/history_3.htm.

5. "The UN Drug Control Conventions: A Primer," by Amira Armenta and Martin Jelsma, Transnational Institute, October 8, 2015, www.tni.org.

6. "Opioid Overdose Crisis," National Institute on Drug Abuse, January 2019, www.drugabuse.gov/drugs-abuse/opioids/opioid-overdose-crisis.

# CHAPTER 1

# Does Medical Research with Illicit Drugs Benefit Patients?

# Studies Document Potential Medicinal Effects of Illicit Substances, but Questions Remain

*Monica Dybuncio and Ryan Jaslow*

*Monica Dybuncio is a New York City–based graphic designer and art director. Ryan Jaslow is the senior public relations director at NYU Langone Medical Center and a writer for CBS News Interactive and WebMD.*

Illicit drugs are bad for you. Almost every doctor will recommend avoiding recreational drug use, because it can lead to long-term health problems and drug abuse that can ruin personal relationships and even send a person to an early grave.

But while drugs can be dangerous, illicit drugs have been researched for centuries, and some have been found to have surprising therapeutic benefits.

Whether it's a psychological benefit or treating an addiction to one drug with the help of another, several studies document the potential medicinal effects of otherwise illegal drugs.

## LSD (Acid)

Lysergic acid diethylamide, known as LSD or acid, comes in tablets, capsules, liquid, or on absorbent paper. The hallucinogenic drug produces "trips" that last about 12 hours and involve unpredictable feelings of panic and fright. Although LSD raises body temperature, heart rate and blood pressure, and has even been linked to "flashbacks" months after use, it may have a sobering effect on alcoholics, according to a recent study.

The study found people with alcohol problems who took LSD reported greater self-acceptance, awareness and motivation to address their alcohol abuse.

"Surprising Medical Uses for Illicit Drugs," by Monica Dybuncio and Ryan Jaslow, CBS Interactive Inc., March 12, 2012. Reprinted by permission.

## Marijuana

The most commonly used illegal drug in the US has found many purposes—recreational, spiritual, and medicinal. Uncle Sam even doles out free joint canisters to four Americans who were grandfathered into an experimental government treatment study that looked at marijuana for medicinal reasons. Others are simply authorized to grow medical marijuana on their own. Marijuana has been found to relieve chronic pain, prevent post-traumatic stress disorder, and has even found celebrity advocates such as TV personality Montel Williams.

Currently 16 US states and Washington D.C. have medical marijuana laws on the books.

But marijuana use has also been tied to long-term brain problems, risk for psychotic symptoms, and deadly car crashes.

## MDMA (Ecstasy)

MDMA, known as ecstasy, XTC or X, is a synthetic drug that produces short-term feelings of emotional warmth, physical energy, and enhanced sensory perception. But it can also cause nausea, chills, muscle cramping and blurred vision. The drug, which grew in popularity as a club drug, was found to potentially hold the key to better treatments for deadly blood cancers such as leukemia, lymphoma, and myeloma.

Another study found MDMA combined with therapy could help treat post-traumatic stress disorder (PTSD).

## Cocaine

Cocaine, known in its crystal form as "crack," is a highly addictive stimulant that is snorted, injected, or smoked. It produces feelings of euphoria while increasing body temperature, blood pressure, and heart rate—thereby also raising risk for heart attacks, respiratory failure, strokes and seizures. Sudden death can occur on the first use of cocaine.

Despite its dangers, cocaine has a history of medicinal use, once used as a stimulant for those wasting away from disease or morphine addiction—the latter was especially common following the Civil War—and thought to be a general cure-all, sold as tonics by pharmacists. Cocaine was also one of the earliest anesthetics used for surgery. Some current anesthetics, such as novocaine, use safer versions of the chemical without the psychological effects.

## Psilocybin (Magic Mushrooms)

Psilocybin is a hallucinogen found in certain kinds of fungus, commonly known as psychedelic or magic mushrooms. While consuming these mushrooms produces short-term drug "trips," research has found that magic mushrooms may lead to a long-term greater sense of well-being and help treat depression.

Another study found the drug could give people a more "open" personality, making them more likely to quit smoking or treat anxiety and depression in cancer patients.

"We're not saying go out there and eat magic mushrooms," Professor David Nutt, a neuropsychopharmacology researcher at Imperial College London and magic mushroom study author said. "But...this drug has such a fundamental impact on the brain that it's got to be meaningful—it's got to be telling us something about how the brain works."

## Ibogaine

Ibogaine is a hallucinogenic drug that's found in African Iboga shrubs and is commonly taken for religious rituals. Despite it being a powerful hallucinogen that's illegal in the US, some addiction doctors in other countries are turning to the plant to treat heroin and opioid addiction.

One ibogaine researcher, Dr. Kenneth Alper of NYU Langone Medical Center, told HealthPop last summer that the approach is mostly used for people who fail more conventional treatments. The drug is thought to work for addicts by helping them through potentially deadly withdrawal symptoms, and reportedly changing drug-seeking behavior in some addicts.

## Ketamine

Ketamine, also known as "Special K," is a club-drug that puts users in a trance-like state known as a "K-hole." The drug is commonly used as a cat tranquilizer by veterinarians, and may cause visual hallucinations, vivid dreams, confusion and disorientation, increased salivation, and problems with heart rhythm and breathing.

But a recent study of depressed patients at Ben Taub General Hospital in Houston found the drug treated people with suicidal depression during the critical stretch when depressed patients were most vulnerable.

"It was a different experience from feeling high. This was feeling that something has been removed," said Dr. Carlos Zarate, a ketamine researcher at the National Institute of Mental Health.

# The Possibilities for Innovative Medical Treatments Are Unlimited

*Phillip Francis*

*Phillip Francis is an author and editor on topics of contemporary importance for the* Cheat Sheet. *His interests focus on public health, wellness, and contemporary life issues.*

For as long as we can remember, drugs were bad, unless of course they were prescribed to you by a doctor to help you with what ails you. Many of us were proud graduates of the DARE program, and still might even have our certificate on the wall.

All those tools we learned in that program were quickly dispelled, after realizing all the information we were taught was wildly inaccurate, and statistically ineffective at preventing drug use. Now to dispel some anxiety, it seems that all these "Evil" drugs that we were taught about in the DARE program have become incredible uses in the field of medicine.

Here are 7 drugs being used in incredible new ways, oftentimes even saving lives.

## CBD Oil from Marijuana Is Used to Treat Chronic Seizures

Cannabis has been used for thousands of years in a medicinal capacity all over the world, but it's only recently when the larger population has started to get back on board with that train of thought. Cannabis has two primary components: Tetrahydrocannabinol (or THC, known as the psychoactive part that gets you high), and cannabidiol, which acts completely separately from THC, and has shown strong effects in treating seizures. It's not fully understood why CBD works, but it does. Studies are being conducted to understand it further.

"Can Illegal Drugs Save Lives? Stunning Studies Point Toward Endless Possibilities," by Phillip Francis, *Cheat Sheet*, November 1, 2017. Reprinted by permission.

## THC Is Being Used in Cancer Treatment

When people get cancer, the standard form of treatment involves chemotherapy. Chemotherapy, while often effective, always comes with a host of horrendous side effects. THC is the counterweight to those side effects. It has been shown to help with nausea and vomiting caused by chemotherapy when smoked. Being able to eat and keep your food down helps tremendously when in such a serious fight for your life. A small number of studies have also shown it to be effective in treating neuropathic pain, or chronic pain from damaged nerves.

## MDMA/Ecstasy Is Being Used to Treat and Cure PTSD

PTSD is an incredibly difficult mental illness to treat, and a good of what has been on the market has just been used to numb the symptoms. What MDMA does for a victim is allow them to look at the event(s) that they have experienced from an outside perspective, and let go of them. Initial studies showed that a large number of people in the trial treatment no longer suffered from symptoms of PTSD before the program was even over. The best part is that patients remain symptom-free for years to come.

## Ketamine Is Being Used for Depression

Yes, we are talking about the horse tranquilizer, or better known on the street as "special K." This drug is being used to treat depression, because it has dissociative qualities that can be helpful in treatment. The truth is that only about 45% of depression sufferers see any improvement in their illness from traditional antidepressants. This is still being studied, but in limited studies, ketamine has shown itself to be far more effective than other options.

## Magic Mushrooms Are Being Used to Treat People with Deep Anxiety

Magic mushrooms are now more than accidental fun time while camping. Researchers are using pure, synthesized psilocybin (the active psychedelic component in mushrooms) to help patients with extreme anxiety issues. In a study conducted by Johns Hopkins University, 80% of patients found clinically significant improvement in their symptoms. A similar study performed by New York University showed similar results. The treatment usually takes just a few hours, and has significant, enduring impacts on the mental health of patients.

## LSD Is Being Used to Be More Productive at Work

LSD has been in the news and gossip columns lately, having recently been shown to improve people's work habits through a method called "micro-dosing." Generally, a subject will take 10 micrograms of LSD every 4 days. It's a very trendy idea, however, the evidence is almost purely anecdotal.

So far there have not been any traditional studies to gauge its effectiveness, but thousands of people across the world have hailed it as a turning point in their lives. Essentially the micro-dosing of the drug creates a serious sharpness that one would get from an extremely restful night, and also allows people to look at the bigger picture of things, rather than focusing on only on the small aspect.

## Heroin Is Being Used to Treat Opioid Addiction

You didn't read that wrong. This is an actual treatment that researchers are looking into. At Hannover Medical School in Germany, Dr. Torsten Passie is using small amounts of heroin to wean addicts off of opioids like Percocet, Vicodin, Demerol, and Oxycontin. His studies have shown that most patients don't even feel the intoxicating effects of heroin after about a month, while other drug use (marijuana, alcohol, and benzodiazepines) was been significantly decreased. After about a year, 60% of the subjects studied had stopped using drugs altogether.

The thing with drugs is that there is always a good and bad side, whether they're a pharmaceutical prescription, or a street drug. The fact remains that there will always be a medical use for many of them, and as such, it would do us well to change our perception and move forward to a better future.

# Drugs from the 1960s Are the Focus of New Research

*Denis Campbell*

*Denis Campbell is the health policy editor for the* Guardian *and the* Observer *in the UK. He has written about the National Health Service, public health, and medicine since 2007.*

A growing number of people are taking LSD and other psychedelic drugs such as cannabis and ecstasy to help them cope with a variety of conditions including anorexia nervosa, cluster headaches and chronic anxiety attacks.

The emergence of a community that passes the drugs between users on the basis of friendship, support and need—with money rarely involved—comes amid a resurgence of research into the possible therapeutic benefits of psychedelics. This is leading to a growing optimism among those using the drugs that soon they may be able to obtain medicines based on psychedelics from their doctor, rather than risk jail for taking illicit drugs.

Among those in Britain already using the drugs and hoping for a change in the way they are viewed is Anna Jones (not her real name), a 35-year-old university lecturer, who takes LSD once or twice a year. She fears that without an occasional dose she will go back to the drinking problem she left behind 14 years ago with the help of the banned drug.

LSD, the drug synonymous with the 1960s counter-culture, changed her life, she says. "For me it was the catalyst to give up destructive behaviour—heavy drinking and smoking. As a student I used to drink two or three bottles of wine, two or three days a week, because I didn't have many friends and didn't feel comfortable in my own skin.

"Scientists Study Possible Health Benefits of LSD and Ecstasy," by Denis Campbell, Guardian News & Media Limited, October 23, 2009. Reprinted by permission.

"Then I took a hit of LSD one day and didn't feel alone any more. It helped me to see myself differently, increase my self-confidence, lose my desire to drink or smoke and just feel at one with the world. I haven't touched alcohol or cigarettes since that day in 1995 and am much happier than before."

Many others are using the drugs to deal with chronic anxiety attacks brought on by terminal illness such as cancer.

Research was carried out in the 1950s and 1960s into psychedelics. In some places they were even used as a treatment for anxiety, depression and addiction. But a backlash against LSD—owing to concerns that the powerful hallucinogen was becoming widespread as a recreational drug, and fear that excessive use could trigger mental health conditions such as schizophrenia—led to prohibition of research in the 1970s.

Under the 1971 Misuse of Drugs Act it is classified as a Class A, schedule 1 substance—which means not only is LSD considered highly dangerous, but it is deemed to have no medical research value.

Now, though, distinguished academics and highly respected institutions are looking again at whether LSD and other psychedelics might help patients. Psychiatrist Dr John Halpern, of Harvard medical school in the US, found that almost all of 53 people with cluster headaches who illegally took LSD or psilocybin, the active compound in magic mushrooms, obtained relief from the searing pain. He and an international team have also begun investigating whether 2-Bromo-LSD, a non-psychedelic version of LSD known as BOL, can help ease the same condition.

Studies into how the drug may be helping such people are also being carried out in the UK. Amanda Feilding is the director of the Oxford-based Beckley Foundation, a charitable trust that investigates consciousness, its altered states and the effects of psychedelics and meditation. She is a key figure in the revival of scientific interest in psychedelics and expresses her excitement about the initial findings of two overseas studies with which her foundation is heavily involved.

"One, at the University of California in Berkeley, was the first research into LSD to get approval from regulators and ethics bodies since the 1970s," she said. Those in the study are the first to be allowed to take LSD legally in decades as part of research into whether it aids creativity. "LSD is a potentially very valuable substance for human health and happiness."

The other is a Swiss trial in which the drug is give alongside psychotherapy to people who have a terminal condition to help them cope with the profound anxiety brought on by impending death. "If you handle LSD with care, it isn't any more dangerous than other therapies," said Dr Peter Gasser, the psychiatrist leading the trial.

At Johns Hopkins University in Washington, another trial is examining whether psilocybin can aid psychotherapy for those with chronic substance addiction who have not been helped by more conventional treatment.

Professor Colin Blakemore, a former chief executive of the Medical Research Council, said the class-A status of psychedelics such as LSD should not stop them being explored as potential therapies. "No drug is completely safe, and that includes medical drugs as well as illegal substances," he said. "But we have well-developed and universally respected methods of assessing the balance of benefit and harm for new medicines.

"If there are claims of benefits from substances that are not regulated medicines—even including illegal drugs—it is important that they should be tested as thoroughly for efficacy and safety as any new conventional drug."

Past reputations may make it hard to get approval for psychedelic medicines, according to the Medicines and Healthcare products Regulatory Agency.

"The known adverse effect profiles of psychedelic drugs would have to be considered very carefully in the risk/benefit analysis before the drugs may be approved for medicinal use," said a spokeswoman. "These products, if approved, are likely to be classified as a prescription-only medicine and also likely to remain on the dangerous drug list, which means that their supply would be strictly controlled."

# Creating Contemporary Criteria for Drug Evaluation and Policies

*Veljko Dubljević*

*Veljko Dubljević is an assistant professor of philosophy and neuro-ethics at North Carolina State University and an associate editor at Frontiers Media.*

Drug scheduling within the international system of drug control and national legislation has been recently criticized as having insufficient footing in scientific evidence. The legal harms related to non-medical uses of certain drugs (e.g., cannabis) have arguably exceeded their physiological and social harmfulness compared to legally available substances (e.g., tobacco), which prompted some states to explore alternative regulation policies, similar to the drug regime in the Netherlands. Other legally prescribed drugs (e.g., stimulants) created a surge of interest for "better than well" uses, while yet others (e.g., opioids) caused an epidemic of dramatic proportions in North America. The evidence-based multi-criteria drug harm scale (MCDHS) has been proposed as a way of grounding policy in the actual degree of harmfulness of drugs. Indeed, the scale has had great ramifications in several areas of policy, and it has been used extensively in distinct lines of interdisciplinary research. However, some aspects of MCDHS remain disputed. For example, the way the data has been generated has been criticized as suffering from "expert bias." This article reviews strengths and weaknesses of evidence provided with the use of MCDHS. Furthermore, the author argues that the shortcomings of MCDHS can be resolved by offering methodological improvements. These include (1) dissociating the harms of use from harms of abuse, (2) adding the perspectives of people who use drugs, pharmacists, and

"Toward an Improved Multi-Criteria Drug Harm Assessment Process and Evidence-Based Drug Policies," by Veljko Dubljević, *Frontiers in Pharmacology*, August 20, 2018. https://www.frontiersin.org/articles/10.3389/fphar.2018.00898/full. Licensed under CC BY 4.0 International.

general medical practitioners along with the expert assessments, and (3) focusing on subsets of drugs to allow for comparison without mixing different social contexts of drug use. The paper concludes with outlines of substance subset-specific extensions of the MCDHS and related policy proposals in the four areas identified as generating the most controversy: non-medical use of opioids, "study aid" uses of stimulants, shifting trends in nicotine containing products, and regulation of medical and recreational uses of cannabis.

## Introduction

It is safe to assert that the international drug control regime is in flux. The lone example of the Netherlands in terms of loosening the control and decriminalizing or legalizing the use of certain illegal drugs presumed to be safer than previously assumed (e.g., cannabis) has recently been followed by certain states in the US, and on the level of national legislation, Uruguay and Canada. On the other hand, legal drugs such as prescription stimulants and opioids, which have been presumed (and regulated as) safe, have turned out to be quite a challenge in terms of public health. Finally, the promise of "safer forms" of nicotine-containing products has been complicated by new "abuse-like" trends in the use of e-cigarettes. This underscores the need to revise the scientific bases of drug control policies, and most notably, the assessment of harm.

Currently, in most jurisdictions, transnational pharmaceutical corporations are funding the studies that provide evidence that new drugs and substances are safe and effective. Even though this might introduce significant bias, such industry-funded studies are necessary since they are very expensive and governments do not have sufficient funds. However, the vested interests of the pharma industry are not the only source of bias. Namely, most countries and international agencies have drug classification systems that purport to be structured according to the post-market monitoring of the relative risks and dangers of psychoactive substances. Details vary from one jurisdiction to another, but some sort of scheduling classification is in use, based on binding international treaties (i.e., the Single Convention on Narcotic Drugs of 1961 as amended by the 1972 Protocol, the Convention on Psychotropic Substances of 1971, and the United Nations Convention against Illicit Traffic in Narcotic Drugs and Psychotropic Substances of 1988). For instance, in the United States, the federal Controlled Substances Act (CSA) provides the rationale for scheduling in terms of "potential for abuse" and "abuse rate" as "a determinate factor in the scheduling of the drug […] Schedule I drugs have a high potential for abuse and the potential to create severe psychological and/or physical dependence. As the drug schedule changes—Schedule II, Schedule III, etc., so does the abuse potential—Schedule V drugs represent the least potential for abuse" (Drug Enforcement Agency [DEA], 2018).

Within the system of international treaties and drug control policies on a national level, scheduling is an important issue, as it determines how drugs and substances are legally regulated—and more importantly, how users of drugs and substances are treated. For instance, cannabis is federally scheduled in the category of drugs and substances with the most potential for abuse (Schedule I), whereas oxycodone (available as a prescription opioid) and amphetamine (available as a prescription stimulant) are ranked as Schedule II and nicotine containing products are not scheduled. Recently, the scheduling of drugs and addictive substances has been criticized as having insufficient footing in scientific evidence. Indeed, some perspectives on the harmfulness of drugs have been informed by ideological—and at times, racist—agendas. For example, the introduction of the key legal controls of drugs (such as the 1914 Harrison Act) was bolstered by playing on public fears of "drug-crazed, sex-mad negroes" that are "murdering whites under the influence of drugs," along with "degenerate Mexicans" smoking marijuana and "Chinamen seducing white women with opium."

Putting past political rhetoric aside, the issue is not whether policy-makers in ages past have been racist, but whether the socially imposed drug harms they helped enact can be justified today. Many experts believe that they cannot. For instance, Fischer and Kendall (2011) claim that drug and substance control systems have little to no footing in scientific evidence and fail to follow elementary principles informed by empirical logic. According to this view, "drug scheduling [...] originated as a tool of socio-economic control of non-white minority groups, and hence the original drugs included successively in the drug control schedule were opium, cocaine and cannabis (1908–1925). The conceptual framework laid then, and which persists today, *had neither public health, nor pharmacology, nor any attempt of rigorous harm quantification as a foundation*" (Fischer and Kendall, 2011, p. 1891 – emphasis added).

Such criticisms may have motivated certain state jurisdictions in the United States to contradict federal law, at least in terms of cannabis regulation. Indeed, a lengthy debate over drug policy has concluded that prohibitive policies seem to be discredited. Most notably, even staunch supporters of drug control agree that the current prohibition regime is too harsh and costly, especially in cases of relatively harmless drugs and substances. However, the problem is how to establish transparent, evidence-based criteria about which drugs and substances are "relatively harmless."

## The Initial Multi-Criteria Drug Harm Scale Proposal

The multi-criteria drug harm scale (MCDHS) has been proposed as a solution to this problem. The idea behind the scale is that qualitative methodology, such as the Delphi method (which entails consulting experts separately to rate drug harms without disclosing the identity of the expert pool in the process) and consensus workshops can provide a platform for a complex and thorough deliberation of the multi-faceted nature of harm from drug and substance use.

According to the original publication detailing the method, a group of United Kingdom-based experts in psychiatry, pharmacology, and addiction used a 4-point scale to rate drugs in three major dimensions of harm: physical health effects, potential for dependence, and social harm, with 0 representing no risk;

(1), some risk; (2), moderate risk; and (3), extreme risk. Before 16 experts met to discuss and provide the final rankings, a first wave of 29 expert responses was analyzed by the study authors and disseminated to the expert workshop participants. The resulting ranking was the end-product of iterative evaluations based on best available evidence: the final numbers represented mean values from multiple assessments.

This methodology promised to offer a systematic framework and process that could be used by national and international regulatory bodies to assess the harm of current and future drugs that have been used for non-medical purposes. However, the harmfulness ranking of drugs produced by this assessment process differed markedly from the assumptions of most regulatory systems.

Namely, the ranking of harmfulness confirmed some of the expectations expressed in the academic debate on drug control: heroin was ranked as the most harmful drug whereas the harm scores of cannabis were much lower than that of currently legal substances, such as tobacco. However, surprisingly, alcohol was initially rated fairly high on the harmfulness range whereas the "psychedelic drug" LSD and the "party drug" MDMA/ecstasy scored very low. The fact that LSD and MDMA are prohibited and strongly regulated substances while alcohol is legally available caused an uproar of public controversy as a reaction to these harm ratings. Additionally, khat, a less well-known stimulant herb traditionally chewed in Yemen, Somalia and Kenya, was initially ranked as the least harmful substance (see next section).

One of the strengths of the MCDHS was that a process of utilizing large areas of knowledge about drugs and potentially addictive substances has been systematized in a transparent manner, which allows for replication, as well as improvement of the methodology. Indeed, a follow up study in the Netherlands was published, and the methodology applied by 19 Dutch experts produced similar results: legal substances such as alcohol and tobacco were rated as drastically more harmful than some illegal drugs such as cannabis and MDMA/ecstasy. The correlation coefficient between the two sets of rankings has been calculated at 0.87, indicating a high degree of reliability and validity. The most harmful substances according to this ranking were crack cocaine, heroin, tobacco and alcohol whereas the least harmful were anabolic steroids, khat, LSD and psilocybin/"magic mushrooms." This study also aimed at improving the MCDHS methodology by (1) introducing shared "fact sheets" on drugs to increase transparency and (2) rating harms at individual and population level. Another strength of MCDHS was that harm rankings provided numerical assessments that could be analyzed in different areas of academic research, in order to provide guidance on specific drug policy proposals. However, the public controversy over harmfulness of alcohol (mentioned above) was not isolated—very soon a lively debate ensued about the methodological usefulness of the approach.

## Criticisms and Objections

Important criticisms have been leveled against the MCDHS on methodological grounds and specific concerns raised in the cases of MDMA/ecstasy and khat. In an illuminating article, Parrott (2007) offered extensive criticism of the specific ratings of the initial scale. First of all, Parrott's analysis revealed that it is probable that some existing drug harms were not perceived by the experts, whereas other harm rankings (such as for alcohol) were driven by outlier populations (e.g., chronic alcohol abusers). For instance, MDMA/ecstasy users report on average 8 physical and 4 psychological problems, which they attribute to their drug use. Also, social drinkers (as opposed to heavy drinkers) are used as healthy control groups in studies of MDMA/ecstasy use. Also, Parrott notes that khat is seldom used in Western societies, whereas certain communities with a cultural tradition of use (mostly in Somalia, Yemen and Kenya, and respective expatriate communities in the West) experience a range of adverse effects, including significant gastro-intestinal distress, with epigastric bloating, abdominal distension and genito-urinary problems. Long term khat-chewing leads to developing oral cancers (similar to tobacco-chewing) and addiction: acute mood gains are followed by adverse withdrawal symptoms, insomnia followed by delayed waking, reduced daily work performance, anorexia, and increased psychiatric distress.

Finally, Parrott states that khat use may be associated with cognitive performance deficits (e.g., 25% of students at a Somali University who were khat chewers had significantly lower academic performance grades, despite coming from higher income families), increased psychosocial distress and financial hardship (e.g., many users in Kenya spend more than half of their domestic budgets on khat).

Thus, it is safe to assume that the lowly rankings of harm for khat and MDMA/ecstasy could be more likely connected to a lack of personal experience (and perhaps relevant data) of the experts in the harmful effects of these specific substances rather than genuine lack of harm. Additional issues that MCDHS failed to address (and was criticized for) are lack of attention to situational factors, value judgments, and input from relevant stakeholders.

As Nutt (2011) rightly notes in his response to critics, the fact that a certain methodology has drawbacks does not mean that it should be entirely abandoned, especially if no alternative has been proposed. However, these important criticisms that have been leveled against the MCDHS on methodological grounds, and specific concerns raised in the cases of MDMA/ecstasy and khat require a critical assessment of the methodology as well as determination of how far the weaknesses of the scale affect the conclusions drawn from it, most notably the policy proposals.

## Updated Methodology: Multi-Criteria Decision Analysis for Evidence-Based Drug Harm Assessment and Policy

In an effort to increase validity of the scale, the lead proponent (David Nutt) founded the Independent Scientific Committee on Drugs in the United Kingdom and repeated the drug harm ratings with a revised methodology based on weighted scores of multi-criteria decision analysis (MCDA) modeling. This introduced the expert assessment not only to raw harmfulness scores but also to relevant importance (or weights) of different harm dimensions. Namely, drugs were scored with points from 0 to 100, with 100 being assigned to the most harmful drug on a specific criterion, and 0 indicating no harm on that particular criterion. Weighting subsequently compared the drugs that scored 100 across all the criteria, thereby expressing the value judgment that some criteria are more important than others. The final list of criteria included Drug-specific mortality, Drug-related mortality, Drug-specific damage, Drug-related damage, Dependence, Drug-specific impairment of mental functioning, Drug-related impairment of mental functioning, Loss of tangibles, Loss of relationships, Injury (to others), Crime, Environmental damage, Family adversities, International damage, Economic cost, and Community (cohesion/reputation). These criteria, with minor alterations to suit the context, have been used in most follow up studies (discussed below).

As with the Netherlands study, the repeated ranking for the UK assessed harms to users (the first nine criteria) and harms to others (the latter seven criteria) and found that alcohol, heroin, crack cocaine and methamphetamine are the most harmful drugs, whereas the least harmful were MDMA/ecstasy, LSD, buprenorphine (an opioid replacement drug) and psilocybin/"magic mushrooms." The harms of alcohol "to others" appear to have disproportionally affected the rating and precipitated the heated exchange in the journal *Addiction*, where some of the critics argued that the "false promise" of an evidence-based policy was ultimately rooted in "false premises" of a deeply flawed methodology.

The lead authors engaged in the two national MCDHS studies (in the United Kingdom and Netherlands, respectively) appeared to be undaunted by the controversy; they joined forces and expanded their scope by creating a Europe-wide expert panel for assessment of drug harms by using the MCDA modeling methodology. The stated goal was to mitigate the fact that a certain drug might be scarcely used in one region of Europe, whereas it is highly used in another region. Again, the rating found that alcohol, heroin, crack cocaine and methamphetamine are the most harmful drugs, whereas the least harmful were anabolic steroids, LSD, buprenorphine and psilocybin. The proponents of the methodology also tried to accommodate some of the deserved criticism in subsequent work by incorporating assessments of well specified substances containing nicotine, prescription opioids used in the United Kingdom, and even by modeling harms of specific drug policies for regulation of alcohol and cannabis.

The study on the harmfulness of nicotine-containing products developed the rating that found cigarettes as most harmful nicotine containing products (100%), followed by small cigars (67%), pipes (22%) and cigars (16%). The least harmful nicotine containing substances were found to be Electronic Nicotine Delivery Systems or ENDS (5%), nasal sprays (3%), Oral Nicotine Delivery Products (2%), and Dermal Nicotine Delivery Products or "patches" (1%). Even though there is little doubt that the three nicotine containing products ranked as least harmful are much safer than traditional tobacco products, there remain doubts whether all ENDS are really safe or if data about their long term harmfulness is simply lacking. Similarly, there are reasons to question whether the sharp drop in harmfulness ratings between small cigars and pipes is more due to lower prevalence of use rather than genuine lack of long-term adverse effects, which would indicate that at least some methodological artifacts are embedded in the research findings (see the discussion on improvements of the methodology below). An additional confound is engendered in the interpretation of data. Does the fact that pipes are rated as more than four times safer than cigarettes, or that ENDS are rated as twenty times safer, mean that public health messages or regulation should incorporate these findings and argue for a change in preferred product in long term nicotine users? Some of the proponents of the MCDHS believed so (most notably David Nutt) and petitioned the Australian Government to change the current scheduling of nicotine containing products if they are ENDS. The petition ultimately failed, but in the public deliberations, expert opinions of the proponents of MCDHS were acknowledged and contrasted to worries that "dripping"—ultimately a drug abuse technique—may be leading to exposure to high nicotine levels.

As was the case with the controversy over policy recommendations regarding alcohol, there are good reasons to consider applying caution in translating research findings directly into policy; the historical record of the failed policy of prohibition in the United States, along with counter-intuitiveness of many findings from the MCDHS/MCDA process, has made many policy makers and commentators reluctant to take heed of the policy recommendations engendered by the methodology. However, there are areas where evidence-based interventions and policy evaluations are desperately needed, at least in the North American context, and these are with opioid and cannabis regulation. As noted above, the MCDA methodology has provided some valuable input, and the transparent nature of the process allows for methodological improvements.

The study on the harmfulness of non-medically used prescription opioids (in the United Kingdom) developed the rating that found injected heroin as most harmful (99%), followed by smoked heroin (70%), fentanyl (55%), and diamorphine (50%). The least harmful prescription opioids were found to be tramadol (16%), suboxone (15%), compound codeine products (12%) and codeine (10%). A surprising finding was that oxycodone was rated as only moderately harmful (22%), even less harmful than methadone (30%). The study authors note on that particular issue that their harmfulness ratings are "not independent of prevalence of use" (Van Amsterdam et al., 2015b, p. 1003) and that the aggressive marketing and promoting of oxycodone in the US could mean that this same substance could be much more dangerous in other populations. Direct to consumer marketing of opioids in the United States could be an additional aspect of social harm that future studies might need to address.

In terms of assessing policy options, MCDA methodology was applied as a new approach to formulate and appraise regulations of alcohol and cannabis. It is hard to determine what effect (if any) this new application of the methodology might have for the future of public policy, but it is fair to assert that the transparency of assessment criteria at least invites informed public debate. The list of 27 criteria grouped into seven thematic clusters included Health (Harm reduction to users, Harm reduction to others, Shift to lower-harm products, Encouraging treatment, Improving product quality), Social (Promoting drug education, Enabling medical use, Promoting research, Protecting human rights, Promoting individual liberty, Improving community cohesion, Promoting family cohesion), Political (Supporting international development or security, Reducing industry influence), Public (Promoting well-being, Protecting the young, Protecting the vulnerable, Respecting religious or cultural values), Crime (Reducing criminalization of users, Reducing acquisitive crime, Reducing violent crime, Preventing corporate crime, Preventing criminal industry), Economic (Generating state revenue, Reducing economics costs), and Costs (Policy introduction costs, Policy maintenance costs).

The four policies rated were free market/"laissez faire," state control, decriminalization, and absolute prohibition. Expert ratings favored state control for both alcohol and cannabis regulation, whereas absolute prohibition was least favored. The major difference was that absolute prohibition of alcohol did garner some support (55%) from experts based on the identified clusters of criteria, whereas absolute prohibition of cannabis garnered minimal support (5%). Again, it is too early to tell if these assessments might guide or are the result of the ongoing "flux" in drug policy proposals, but undeniably, past regulatory approaches have been motivated by 'extreme solutions' that failed to address the full set of relevant issues.

The MCDHS/MCDA methodology appears to have provided at least some robust results in terms of reliability and validity and allows for breaking down complex evaluations into a series of smaller, more easily assessed issues. However, many methodological issues remain unresolved (see next section), and the question of objective replicability looms large. Namely, although the proponents of the methodology boast of a high overall correlation in follow-up replication studies, these are not independent studies; key proponents of the model have been active in the studies, and most of the time, only European experts have been involved in the ratings. Thus, independent replication is still lacking. Indeed, as Van Amsterdam and colleagues have noted, "it would be of interest to repeat [the] MCDA harm assessment in the United States," but the scientific and public interests would best be served if this was done using an improved methodology and by unrelated researchers in North and South America and followed up by similar assessments elsewhere in the world.

## Remaining Methodological Artifacts and Blind-Spots

The major obstacle to the adequate assessment of harm is the reification of substance harms without allowing for the differential recognition of context of use. Namely, the greatest controversy surrounded the classification of alcohol as the most harmful substance in the European rating of drug harms. This result undermined the face validity of the methodology and at the same time offers clues as to how the method can be improved. The relatively high incidence of fatal drunk-driving accidents and health issues connected to long-term alcohol abuse have pushed the harmfulness rating for alcohol over those of heroin and crack cocaine. Yet, social drinkers (as used as control groups in drug abuse studies) can and do drink responsibly. The point is not that alcohol is not potentially dangerous or that there aren't harms associated even with "responsible use" of alcohol, but that the social context of use matters. For instance, hydration is essential for survival, and at the same time, overuse of hydration can be deadly. This underscores the need to provide multiple assessments for harm: harms of regular, low-dose use, and harms of overuse and abuse.

Furthermore, it is clear that the alleged "universal knowledge" of experts has specific blind spots, most notably in terms of substances where they lack personal experience. This is where the "local knowledge" of people who use these drugs might be beneficial in correcting the "expert bias." Certainly, science often outstrips common sense experience and is essential for identifying phenomena that are not immediately perceptible to people. However, consulting expert opinions of scientists does not guarantee that assessments will be correct, especially with phenomena that have an important social component. For example, psychiatry experts consulted prior to the Stanford prison experiment and the Milgram experiments not only failed to predict the extent to which negative behaviors would take place, but their expert opinions were so widely off the mark so as to designate some of the most harmful psychological experiments in known history as harmless. Therefore, additional safeguards for objectivity and stakeholder perspectives are necessary to provide relevant input in the assessment procedure, and any assessment results need to be acknowledged as provisional and revisable based on new evidence. In this respect, adding the perspectives of people who use drugs, pharmacists, and general medical practitioners along with the expert assessments might need to be the new "gold standard" for substance harm assessment.

Finally, the policy analysis of different potentially addictive substances should take into account the source of the substance in question. For instance, a policy analysis of stimulants might need to have at least two separate harm assessments for many of the drugs in question. Namely, taking into consideration the differences between say prescription amphetamines (such as Adderall, the purity of which is controlled) and street amphetamines (to which additional harmful substances are often added) seems to be a *conditio sine qua non* of successful application of the methodology.

## The Way Forward

Having a transparent methodology for providing an evidence base for drug policy which still needs to be perfected is better than having no methodology at all. After the careful analysis of the strengths and weaknesses of the MCDHS/MCDA methodology, it is important to identify areas of drug/substance harms that need to be urgently (re)assessed. Given that the current major issues with the public health concerns are related to increased opioid and stimulant use, shifts in nicotine use, and cannabis regulation, it makes sense to make the assessment of harms in these categories with the improved methodology a priority.

The reassessment of opioids might provide valuable data that at the same time validates and expands on the previous results. Namely, it could be the case that the moderate harmfulness rating of oxycodone is actually correct in assessing harms of regular, low dose use, whereas the separate harmfulness ranking of non-medical use might provide decision makers and physicians with valuable evidence that would guide better crafted drug policies. Furthermore, dissociating between the harms (e.g., in terms of Drug-specific mortality) of the substance in question from different sources and grades of purity might provide input for harm reduction strategies that do not cause undue social and legal burdens. Most notably, these should not be based on expert assessments alone, but informed by perspectives from people who use drugs, pharmacists, and general medical practitioners. Multiple iterative rankings prior to final expert ranking should be the 'gold standard' in harm assessments. Finally, expanding the list of criteria to include the perception of certain benefits of regular, low dose use (e.g., Promoting well-being in populations experiencing chronic or acute pain) and perception of specific social factors (e.g., Social influence of the industry) might broaden the knowledge pool that informs expert assessments. These suggestions are only tentative, and it is up to multiple groups of workshop participants to make value judgments in terms of inclusion and relative relevance of any single criterion.

Similarly, the assessment of stimulants might provide an important addition to the debate over an epidemic that is happening in the shadow of the opioid crisis: the misuse of prescription stimulants in populations of researchers, employees, and students. Prior policy proposals have been taking into account the results from the initial scale ranking, but increased awareness about harmfulness of amphetamines has led to a shift in preference among some student populations and even medical practitioners to newer, atypical stimulant drugs such as modafinil. The fact that newer drugs with stimulant-like properties were not rated at all in any of the MCHDS studies significantly limits the debate on evidence based policy options for this class of drugs. Herbal stimulants with amphetamine-like effects such as khat should be reassessed and contrasted not to a generalized list of drugs, but in a narrowed down scope, to similar substances. Furthermore, dissociating between the harms (e.g., in terms of Dependence) of the substance in question from different sources and grades of purity might provide input for public policies that target specific avenues of drug diversion, which might relieve undue social and legal burdens (e.g., should a student that shared their prescription ADHD medication be treated as a drug dealer?). This analysis would also need to explicitly distinguish between safe recreational users of stimulants and unsafe recreational abusers of stimulants, and it would need to include task-specific benefits for users of stimulants (e.g., in terms of "cognitive enhancement"). Additionally, the criteria need to include explicitly social benefits of use (e.g., Respecting cultural values in khat use). Although any results of the MCDHS/MCDA methodology have to be interpreted with caution, these ratings are the only available and feasible measure of the safety profiles of stimulants, and as such will benefit multiple societies.

The reassessment of nicotine containing products could likewise provide valuable data that at the same time validates and expands on the previous results. Adding the perspectives of (past) users, e-cigarette retailers, and physicians could clarify whether the harms of pipe use and abuse are drastically lower than harms of cigarette use and abuse in terms of specific health outcomes as they are subjectively perceived, and at the same time, they could provide an insight into potential targets for public education and current gaps in evidence. For instance, the current expert rating might have properly rated harms of "cigarette abuse" and "pipe use," thereby confounding their actual harmfulness. Similarly, differentiating forms of use and abuse of ENDS or e-cigarettes might clarify the conflicting expert opinions in terms of ENDS policy. Additionally, probing the perceived social influence of traditional tobacco vs. e-cigarette industry and retailers might benefit the informed public discussions on appropriate harm reduction and discourage use policies and inform targeted taxation efforts that avoid the pitfalls of "regulatory capture."

Finally, a reassessment of cannabis policies should incorporate a comparative study not only of policy types, but also of specific existing policies (including those at the national level, such as the Netherlands, Uruguay, and Canada, and at the State level such as Colorado, Vermont, California, etc.) along with known Health, Social, Political, Public, Law enforcement, and Economic effects. The inclusion of additional perspectives (i.e., people who grow and/or use cannabis and treating physicians) would drastically reduce bias in this volatile and value laden debate. Explicitly distinguishing between recreational uses of cannabis and recreational abuses of cannabis and including specific medical benefits for certain populations (in terms of e.g., chronic pain management) would provide a better evidence base for effective evaluation of public policy.

In conclusion, researchers have a duty to take heed of methodological improvements and initiate assessments of harms within diverse communities and expert groups. At the same time, decision makers and regulators need to better acknowledge and fund such efforts in order to discharge their mandate to the public. Ultimately, further discussion is needed in order to generate as many proposals for evidence based methodological approaches and specific models of drug harm assessment as possible. This is a necessary step in order to provide desperately needed evidence for legislators at federal, state and local levels, prosecutors making decisions in cases of illegal use of drugs and citizens engaged in drug policy change via initiative and referenda activities. Drugs and potentially addictive substances will be adequately regulated only as a result of a public discussion on a sufficiently large, eligible set of evidence based harm assessments and policy options.

# Challenges with Medical Tourism

*Jennifer Whitlock*

*Jennifer Whitlock is a board-certified family practice nurse practitioner (FNP-C) who works as a hospitalist providing care for patients who are recovering from surgery or with illnesses requiring hospitalization.*

Medical tourism, also known as international surgery or surgery abroad, is the process of leaving your home country in order to have treatment in another country. This should not be confused with having an unplanned surgery in a foreign country due to an unexpected illness or injury. Medical tourism means intentionally going to another country for the purpose of having healthcare or surgery.

At this time, it is estimated that 750,000 or more Americans will seek healthcare outside of the United States in the next year. Many of those will be seeking surgery at a lower cost, or a procedure that they are unable to have at home.

## Why Medical Tourism Is So Popular

Medical tourism is appealing for a wide variety of reasons, ranging from the cost of surgery at home, to being an immigrant who prefers to have surgery in their country of origin.

### Lower Costs of Medical Tourism

In fact, the cost of some procedures can be 90 percent less in foreign countries than it would be in the United States. Surgery in India is particularly inexpensive, and patients are flocking to Malaysia, Brazil, Singapore, Costa Rica, Mexico, Thailand, and Vietnam.

We know why surgery in the United States is so expensive, but why is medical and surgical care overseas much cheaper? The cost of labor, whether it is nurses, aides, surgeons or pharmacists, is

"Risks and Benefits of Medical Tourism," by Jennifer Whitlock, Verywell Health, About, Inc., December 31, 2018. Reprinted by permission.

often dramatically lower. Also, malpractice insurance, which can top $250,000 for some specialties, is significantly lower abroad. When the cost of labor is low, everything is less expensive, from the building where care is provided to the cost of meals provided in the hospital.

### Insurance Incentives

Some insurance companies have started promoting medical tourism due to the dramatic savings. Blue Cross and Blue Shield has started a program where the patient has an assigned case manager who will arrange for travel and accommodations for both the patient and a companion of their choosing. The case manager makes arrangements for their medical care, and even arranges for postoperative care, if necessary, at home. Savings for the insurer means savings for the insured.

Some insurance companies offer financial incentives for surgery abroad, discounting or eliminating the percentage of the cost that the patient is expected to pay.

Other insurance companies will not pay for surgery performed outside of the country unless it is an emergency.

### Luxury and Private Nursing

Some patients are drawn to the spa-like luxury that some foreign hospitals offer, seeing the opportunity to be pampered as an additional benefit of inexpensive surgery. Some facilities offer hospital rooms that are more like a hotel suite than a traditional hospital room. Other hospitals offer one on one private nursing care, which is far more generous and attentive than the staffing ratios that most hospitals allow.

### Vacation in a Foreign Country

It sounds wonderful, doesn't it? Your insurance company flying you to an exotic location on the other side of the world? Why not experience a vacation in a foreign country along with surgery?

A vacation is often scheduled immediately before or after surgery, taking advantage of the stay in a foreign country to travel for pleasure. This is an especially inexpensive way to travel to a foreign country if the insurance company is paying for the flight and the cost of staying is low. It seems logical to recover on a beach or at a beautiful location, especially when the cost of staying is often inexpensive when compared to staying home. Just remember, swimming isn't recommended until your incisions are completely closed, and you may not feel up to doing much more than napping in the days following your procedure.

### Bypassing Rules and Regulations

Some travelers seek surgery abroad to bypass rules that are set in place by their own government, insurance company, or hospital. These rules are typically in place to protect the patient from harm, so getting around them isn't always the best idea.

For example, a patient may be told that their weight is too low (healthy) to qualify for weight loss surgery. A surgeon in a foreign country may have a different standard for who qualifies for weight loss surgery, so the patient may qualify overseas for the procedure they want. This is especially true with transplant tourism (more on that later).

### Talented Surgeons

Surgeons in certain countries are often known for their talent in a specific area of surgery. Brazilian surgeons are often touted for their strong plastic surgery skills, and they have ample practice, as Brazilians are rumored to be more likely to have plastic surgery than people from almost any other country. Thailand is reported to be the primary medical tourism destination for individuals seeking gender reassignment. It is often easier to qualify for surgery and the cost is significantly reduced, and the surgeons are performing the procedures frequently, which can lead to improved skill.

It is often surprising to many medical tourists that their physician was trained in the United States. Not all physicians are, of course, but a surprisingly high percentage of them working in surgery abroad are trained in English-speaking medical schools and residency programs and then return to their home country.

These physicians often speak multiple languages and may be board certified in their home country and a foreign country, such as the United States.

Remember, medical tourism isn't limited to countries outside of the United States. Many individuals seek care in different areas of the United States because of the cutting edge technology that is available, as well as the safety of the healthcare and prescription medicine supply.

## Medical Tourism Sounds Wonderful, So What's the Catch?

As wonderful as medical tourism sounds, there are some issues that should be considered prior to signing up to have your medical or surgical treatment in a foreign country. The financial benefits are well known, but the downsides can be significant, even deadly in some cases.

### Poor Quality Surgery Is a Possibility

Just as there are great surgeons abroad, there are also some surgeons that are far less talented. It is often hard to obtain information about physicians and the quality of their work from afar. In the United States, it is often easy to obtain information about malpractice lawsuits, sanctions by medical boards, and other disciplinary actions against a physician. This information may not be as readily available with foreign providers and may make choosing a great surgeon more difficult.

A physician should be trained in the specific area of medicine that is appropriate for your medical and surgical needs. You should not be having plastic surgery from a surgeon who was trained to be a heart doctor, nor should you be having surgery performed by someone who isn't trained as a surgeon. It isn't good enough to be a physician, the physician must be trained in the specialty.

Prior to agreeing to surgery, you should know your surgeon's credentials: where they studied, where they trained, and in what specialty(s) they are board certified. Do not rely on testimonials from previous patients, these are easily made up for a website and even if they are correct, one good surgery doesn't mean they will all be good.

Many American plastic surgeons have spent countless hours repairing the scars and disfiguring surgical damage done by a surgeon in a foreign country. A quick search on the internet will quickly provide hundreds of photos and stories of individuals who were permanently harmed by a foreign surgeon. Poorly trained surgeons, or even well-trained surgeons using poor quality materials, can lead to a terrible final outcome.

### Quality of Staff

Nurses are a very important part of healthcare, and the care they provide can mean the difference between a great outcome and a terrible one. A well-trained nurse can identify a potential problem and fix it before it truly becomes an issue. A poorly trained nurse may not identify a problem until it is too late. The quality of the nursing staff will have a direct impact on your care.

### Quality of the Facility

Is the facility where your surgery will be performed state of the art, or is it dirty, with old equipment, outdated technology, and minimal resources? Is the hospital prepared to help you if you are very ill after surgery or will you need to be sent to a different facility for a higher level of care? Will the surgery be performed in a hospital or a surgical center that is isolated and far away from a major hospital?

These questions are important and should be answered before choosing a facility for surgery. The facility you use should either be a hospital with ICU level care (in case there is a problem during your surgery or recovery) or it should be near a major hospital with the ability to transfer you quickly.

Look for a facility that has an international accreditation, such as Joint Commission International. The Joint Commission is the certifying body of hospitals in the United States, determining if hospitals are providing adequate care or if there are deficiencies. The international division does the same for hospitals outside the United States, and to be certified is a mark of quality.

### Flying Home After Surgery

There is a risk of blood clots after surgery, and flying home, especially on a long haul flight, increases the risk of clots. If the flight home is a long one, plan on getting up and walking up and down the aisles each hour. Try to avoid flying home in the days immediately after surgery; waiting a week will decrease the chances of developing a blood clot or another serious complication during the flight.

### Different Food

If you have a sensitive stomach, you may want to think long and hard about having surgery abroad. The food is often very different in foreign hospitals, and in some areas, there is a risk that even the water will be upsetting to your body. Having diarrhea or postoperative nausea and vomiting can be terrible after surgery, especially if it is made worse by the food you are eating on a daily basis.

### Language Barrier

If you are having surgery in a country where English is not the primary language, you will need to make preparations in order to be able to communicate with the staff. You may be pleasantly surprised to learn that the staff speaks your primary language beautifully. If not, then you will need to consider how you will make your wishes and needs known to the surgeon, the staff, and others you will meet.

## Hope For the Best, Prepare For the Worst

Imagine you go abroad for surgery and during the surgery there is a mistake. For example, the surgeon accidentally cuts a small area of your bowel during your procedure. It may not seem like a big deal, but two days later you are critically ill with an infection that is barely being controlled by IV antibiotics. You need to return to surgery to repair the mistake. If you do not get better, you will need to be moved to the ICU, and you may need to be on a ventilator until your condition improves.

In a hospital in the United States, this level of care is widely available. Most hospitals have an intensive care unit, and patients who need to be transferred to a larger hospital can be. Imagine this happening during your treatment overseas. Does the facility have an ICU? Does the fee you are paying cover unexpected events like this or will there be an additional cost? Can you afford to get home if your life depends on it? Does your trip include medical travel insurance, which is a type of malpractice coverage that helps with the costs associated with medical mistakes? Does your trip include repatriation insurance, a type of insurance that pays for medical staff to pick you up in a foreign country and return you to your home country with medical care while in flight?

Finding out the answers to these questions, and making sure a high level of care is readily available, will lead to a safer tourism experience, knowing that you will be cared for in the event of an emergency.

## Follow-Up Care

It is important to arrange for your follow-up care prior to leaving your home country. Many physicians and surgeons are hesitant to take care of a patient who received care outside the country, as they are often unfamiliar with medical tourism and have concerns about the quality of care overseas. Arranging for follow-up care before you leave will make it easier to transition to care at home with the stress of trying to find a physician after surgery.

## A Few Words About Organ Transplant Tourism

Transplant tourism is one area of medical tourism that is strongly discouraged by transplant professionals in multiple countries. Most international transplants are considered "black market" surgeries that are not only poor in quality, but ethically and morally wrong. There are significant health-related issues along with more philosophical issues with international transplants.

China, the country that is believed to perform more international kidney transplants than any other country, is widely believed to take organs from political prisoners after their execution. In India, living donors are often promised large sums of money for their kidney donation, only to find out they have been scammed and never receive payment. Selling an organ in India is illegal, as it is in most areas of the world, so there is little recourse for the donor.

Then there is the final outcome, how well the organ works after the surgery is complete. With black market transplants, less care is often taken with matching the donor and recipient, which leads to high levels of rejection. Researchers in Canada found that transplant tourists were three to four times more likely to die or reject a transplanted organ than those who received an organ after being on the waiting list.

Many individuals feel that they are doing the necessary thing and that they will not survive if they are forced to remain on the waiting list for a transplant. The opposite may be true, as some recipients come home with a new organ and a new disease. Cytomegalovirus, tuberculosis, hepatitis B and hepatitis C are common. It is often the new disease that leads to death, rather than the loss of the organ to rejection.

Transplant surgeons are often reluctant to care for a patient after transplant surgery with an unknown physician, a patient who intentionally circumvented the donor process in the United States. Ethics aside, the low quality of surgical skill found in black market transplant surgeons, compounded by the high risk of infection, complication, and rejection makes the transplant tourist a difficult patient to treat. Knowing that someone may have been murdered to obtain the organ is a complicating factor that many surgeons refuse to look past.

Before you finalize your decision, make sure to consider all of these factors and ask the right questions so that you can seamlessly receive the care you deserve.

CHAPTER 2

# Is the Current Drug Approval and Regulation Process the Best Option for Patients?

# A Century of Regulated Drug Development Has Improved Health Outcomes and Created Guidelines for Innovation and New Therapies

*US Food and Drug Administration*

*The US Food and Drug Administration (FDA) is responsible for protecting public health by ensuring the safety, efficacy, and security of human and veterinary drugs, biological products, and medical devices, and by ensuring the safety of the nation's food supply, cosmetics, and products that emit radiation.*

American consumers benefit from having access to the safest and most advanced pharmaceutical system in the world. The main consumer watchdog in this system is FDA's Center for Drug Evaluation and Research (CDER).

The center's best-known job is to evaluate new drugs before they can be sold. CDER's evaluation not only prevents quackery, but also provides doctors and patients the information they need to use medicines wisely. The center ensures that drugs, both brand-name and generic, work correctly and that their health benefits outweigh their known risks.

Drug companies seeking to sell a drug in the United States must first test it. The company then sends CDER the evidence from these tests to prove the drug is safe and effective for its intended use. A team of CDER physicians, statisticians, chemists, pharmacologists, and other scientists reviews the company's data and proposed labeling. If this independent and unbiased review establishes that a drug's health benefits outweigh its known risks, the drug is approved for sale. The center doesn't actually test drugs itself, although it does conduct limited research in the areas of drug quality, safety, and effectiveness standards.

"Development & Approval Process (Drugs)," US Food and Drug Administration. Reprinted by permission.

Before a drug can be tested in people, the drug company or sponsor performs laboratory and animal tests to discover how the drug works and whether it's likely to be safe and work well in humans. Next, a series of tests in people is begun to determine whether the drug is safe when used to treat a disease and whether it provides a real health benefit.

## FDA Approval: What It Means

FDA approval of a drug means that data on the drug's effects have been reviewed by CDER, and the drug is determined to provide benefits that outweigh its known and potential risks for the intended population. The drug approval process takes place within a structured framework that includes:

- *Analysis of the target condition and available treatments*—FDA reviewers analyze the condition or illness for which the drug is intended and evaluate the current treatment landscape, which provide the context for weighing the drug's risks and benefits. For example, a drug intended to treat patients with a life-threatening disease for which no other therapy exists may be considered to have benefits that outweigh the risks even if those risks would be considered unacceptable for a condition that is not life threatening.
- *Assessment of benefits and risks from clinical data*—FDA reviewers evaluate clinical benefit and risk information submitted by the drug maker, taking into account any uncertainties that may result from imperfect or incomplete data. Generally, the agency expects that the drug maker will submit results from two well-designed clinical trials, to be sure that the findings from the first trial are not the result of chance or bias. In certain cases, especially if the disease is rare and multiple trials may not be feasible, convincing evidence from one clinical trial may be enough. Evidence that the drug will benefit the target population should outweigh any risks and uncertainties.

- *Strategies for managing risks*—All drugs have risks. Risk management strategies include an FDA-approved drug label, which clearly describes the drug's benefits and risks, and how the risks can be detected and managed. Sometimes, more effort is needed to manage risks. In these cases, a drug maker may need to implement a Risk Management and Mitigation Strategy (REMS).

Although many of the FDA's risk-benefit assessments and decisions are straightforward, sometimes the benefits and risks are uncertain and may be difficult to interpret or predict. The agency and the drug maker may reach different conclusions after analyzing the same data, or there may be differences of opinion among members of the FDA's review team. As a science-led organization, FDA uses the best scientific and technological information available to make decisions through a deliberative process.

### Accelerated Approval

In some cases, the approval of a new drug is expedited. Accelerated Approval can be applied to promising therapies that treat a serious or life-threatening condition and provide therapeutic benefit over available therapies. This approach allows for the approval of a drug that demonstrates an effect on a "surrogate endpoint" that is reasonably likely to predict clinical benefit, or on a clinical endpoint that occurs earlier but may not be as robust as the standard endpoint used for approval. This approval pathway is especially useful when the drug is meant to treat a disease whose course is long, and an extended period of time is needed to measure its effect. After the drug enters the market, the drug maker is required to conduct post-marketing clinical trials to verify and describe the drug's benefit. If further trials fail to verify the predicted clinical benefit, FDA may withdraw approval.

Since the Accelerated Approval pathway was established in 1992, many drugs that treat life-threatening diseases have successfully been brought to market this way and have made a significant impact on disease course. For example, many antiretroviral drugs used to treat HIV/AIDS entered the market via accelerated approval, and subsequently altered the treatment paradigm. A number of targeted cancer-fighting drugs also have come onto the market through this pathway.

## Drug Development Designations

The agency also employs several approaches to encourage the development of certain drugs, especially drugs that may represent the first available treatment for an illness, or ones that have a significant benefit over existing drugs. These approaches, or designations, are meant to address specific needs, and a new drug application may receive more than one designation, if applicable. Each designation helps ensure that therapies for serious conditions are made available to patients as soon as reviewers can conclude that their benefits justify their risks.

- Fast Track is a process designed to facilitate the development and advance the review of drugs that treat serious conditions, and fill an unmet medical need, based on promising animal or human data. Fast tracking can get important new drugs to the patient earlier. The drug company must request the Fast Track process.
- Breakthrough Therapy designation expedites the development and review of drugs that are intended to treat a serious condition, and preliminary clinical evidence indicates that the drug may demonstrate substantial improvement over available therapy. A drug with Breakthrough Therapy designation is also eligible for the Fast Track process. The drug company must request a Breakthrough Therapy designation.
- Priority Review means that FDA aims to take action on an application within six months, compared to 10 months under standard review. A Priority Review designation directs attention and resources to evaluate drugs that would significantly improve the treatment, diagnosis, or prevention of serious conditions.

# The 2018 FDA Approvals Benefit Patients

*Monique Ellis*

*Monique Ellis is a content marketing consultant in the life sciences industry. She is also an editor and writer of topical life sciences industry news, including guidebooks and white papers focused on contemporary issues affecting professionals in the biological and natural science industries.*

From the first approved cannabis-based drug to the first antibiotic to be developed in over a decade, 2018 has truly been a year of "firsts" in FDA approvals. Surpassing last year's impressive figures, the FDA has approved a record 55 novel drugs, as well as several innovative devices and diagnostics.

Building on their mission in 2017, the FDA has continued to push through treatments for rare and orphan diseases to tackle this key area of unmet medical need. There has also been more effective therapies emerging for life-threatening infectious diseases like HIV, as well as significant steps in combatting the global antibiotic resistance emergency. Among them are certainly some unexpected approvals, such as TPOXX, a drug specifically developed to protect us against the smallpox virus being used in biological warfare.

ProClinical has reviewed the many FDA approvals of 2018 and picked out some of the most innovative and significant of the year:

## Epidiolex (cannabidiol)

Epidiolex is the first FDA-approved drug to contain cannabis. GW Pharmaceuticals gained regulatory approval in June 2018 for the drug which is a purified version of cannabidiol (CBD), one of the many molecules found in marijuana. Epidiolex will used to treat two very rare but severe forms of epilepsy, Lennox-Gastaut Syndrome (LGS) and Dravet syndrome. This marks a big medical

"The Most Significant FDA Approvals of 2018," by Monique Ellis, ProClinical Recruitment, December 12, 2018. Reprinted by permission.

advancement as the active ingredients in marijuana have the potential to lead to many more important discoveries. Epidiolex is predicted to become GW Pharmaceuticals' first blockbuster drug.

## TPOXX (tecovirimat)

Although the historically devastating virus smallpox was declared eradicated by the World Health Organisation (WHO) in 1980, there have been ongoing concerns that the disease could be recreated and used as a bioweapon. In an effort to combat bioterrorism, the US Congress began taking proactive steps with the approval of TPOXX, the first treatment developed specifically to treat smallpox.

Smallpox was thought to kill about 30% of its victims and was one of the leading causes of death in the 18th and 19th centuries. There have been several cases of smallpox being used as biological warfare throughout history, so TPOXX could be key in managing future public health emergencies.

## Lucemyra (lofexidine hydrochroride)

The US is currently experiencing an opioid epidemic, with over 72,000 overdose deaths reported in 2017. Opioids include illegal drugs such as heroin or fentanyl but also medically prescribed painkillers like morphine. Lucemyra is the first non-opioid treatment to be approved by the FDA for the management of withdrawal symptoms following abrupt discontinuation of the drugs. This is US WorldMeds' innovative approach to combatting the opioid epidemic in the most safe and effective way for patients.

Another non-narcotic solution to the crisis is DyAnsys' development of a wearable auricular neurostimulation device called Drug Relief. The device, which gained FDA approval in June 2018, is specifically designed to treat opioid withdrawal symptoms when worn over a 120 hour period. Patients are thought to experience reduced withdrawal within 30-60 minutes of treatment.

## Erleada (apalutamide)

Prostate cancer is the most common cancer and the second leading cause of death in men. There are over 150,000 new cases per year in the US and 40,000 in the UK. Erleada is the first approved drug for the treatment of patients with a particular form of the disease: non-metastatic castration-resistant prostate cancer (NM-CRPC). The drug was granted a Priority review following clinical data showing a 72% reduction in the disease spreading or causing death. Patients who trialled the drug had a median metastasis-free (when the cancer doesn't spread) survival of over two years.

## Crysvita (burosumab-twza)

In recent years, the number of therapies approved for the treatment of orphan and rare disease is on the rise. This is an effort to bring life-saving treatment to the 30 million people suffering from a rare disease in the US alone. According to a report by Evaluate Group, sales of orphan drugs are set to climb 11% each year until 2024.

Key examples of rare disease approvals in 2018 include Crysvita, to treat X-linked hypophosphatemia (XLH), a rare hereditary bone disease. Also, Galafold, the first oral treatment for patients with Fabry disease, a genetic condition caused by the deficiency of an enzyme which often affects the kidneys, heart and nervous system.

## Aimovig (erenumab-aooe)

It's thought that as many as 1 in 7 people in the US suffer from migraines, which are severe headaches that often cause nausea and serious vision problems. Novartis' Aimovig is thought to be ground-breaking for long-suffering migraine patients. It is the only drug to have been specifically developed for migraine prevention and is the very first to block the calcitonin gene-related peptide receptor (CGRP-R), a leading cause of migraines. Clinical trial data reported a 50% or more reduction in monthly migraines, and 1 in 4 were migraine-free after extended use of the drug.

## Apple ECG watch

Apple released the long-awaited Apple Watch Series 4 in December 2018, which includes a very special new electrocardiogram (ECG) feature that has the potential to save lives. The integrated ECG monitor enables people to track their heart rhythm and, crucially, alert them to potentially serious heart conditions like atrial fibrillation (AFib). AFib is an irregular heartbeat that can lead to blood clots, heart attacks and strokes.

The FDA granted clearance of the ECG feature along with another that tracks irregular rhythms. Within the first few days of ECG watch's release there were reports of its effectiveness, alerting users to the condition and urging them to seek life-saving medical attention much sooner.

## Biktarvy (bictegravir, embitcitabine, tenofovir alafenamide)

Biktarvy was a highly anticipated treatment for HIV-1 that finally gained FDA approval in July 2018. It is now the smallest single-tablet treatment for HIV-1 that includes the new integrase inhibitor, bictegravir, combined with tried and tested drugs. Gilead's "complete regime" has shown to be effective in patients both new to therapy and those switching therapies. Clinical trials continue as the efficacy of Biktarvy is tested among women, adolescents and children with HIV.

## Nuzyra (omadacycline)

Antibiotic resistance is one of the fastest growing threats to our health, as antibiotics become less effective in the wake of deadly superbugs. Life science companies are working hard to protect our future health by developing new antibiotics that work against drug-resistant bacteria. In October 2018, the FDA approved Paratek Pharmaceuticals' Nuzyra, a new antibiotic to treat acute bacterial skin infections and community-acquired pneumonia. Significantly, the drug is effective against drug-resistant bacteria like doxycycline.

It's also the first once-daily IV and oral antibiotic to be approved in over a decade.

## Trogarzo (ibalizumab-uiyk)

Like bacteria, viruses can become resistant to drugs. This is certainly the case with the HIV virus. In October 2018, TaiMed Biologics gained FDA-approval for their HIV therapy that offers effective therapy for patients who have a long history of treatment and now find their regimens ineffective due to drug-resistance. Trogarzo marks the beginning of a new class of antiretroviral drugs which are effective against multi drug-resistant HIV, and will provide a life line for patients living with this terrible disease.

2018 has been another strong year for FDA approvals, with many innovative drugs and devices being made available for patients in the USA.

# The Medical Impact of Recent Advances in Technology

*Monique Ellis*

*Monique Ellis is a content marketing consultant in the life sciences industry. She is also an editor and writer of topical life sciences industry news, including guidebooks and white papers focused on contemporary issues affecting professionals in the biological and natural science industries.*

Technology and medicine have gone hand and hand for many years. Consistent advances in pharmaceuticals and the medical field have saved millions of lives and improved many others. As the years pass by and technology continues to improve, there is no telling what advances will come next. Here are the top 10 new medical technologies in 2019:

## Smart Inhalers

Inhalers are the main treatment option for asthma and if taken correctly, will be effective for 90% of patients. However, in reality, research shows that only about 50% of patients have their condition under control and as many as 94% don't use inhalers properly.

To help asthma sufferers to better manage their condition, Bluetooth-enabled smart inhalers have been developed. A small device is attached to the inhaler which records the date and time of each dose and whether it was correctly administered. This data is then sent to the patients' smartphones so they can keep track of and control their condition. Clinical trials showed that using the smart inhaler device used less reliever medicine and had more reliever-free days.

"Top 10 New Medical Technologies of 2019," by Monique Ellis, ProClinical Recruitment, February 27, 2019. Reprinted by permission.

## Robotic Surgery

Robotic surgery is used in minimally invasive procedures and helps to aid in precision, control and flexibility. During robotic surgery, surgeons can perform very complex procedures that are otherwise either highly difficult or impossible. As the technology improves, it can be combined with augmented reality to allow surgeons to view important additional information about the patient in real time while still operating. While the invention raises concerns that it will eventually replace human surgeons, it is likely to be used only to assist and enhance surgeons' work in the future.

## Wireless Brain Sensors

Thanks to plastics, medical advances have allowed scientists and doctors to team up and create bioresorbable electronics that can be placed in the brain and dissolve when they are no longer needed, according to Plasticstoday.com. This medical device will aid doctors in measuring the temperature and pressure within the brain. Since the sensors are able to dissolve, they reduce the need for additional surgeries.

## 3-D Printing

If you haven't heard, 3-D printers have quickly become one of the hottest technologies on the market. These printers can be used to create implants and even joints to be used during surgery. 3-D-printed prosthetics are increasingly popular as they are entirely bespoke, the digital functionalities enabling them to match an individual's measurements down to the millimetre. The allows for unprecedently levels of comfort and mobility.

The use of printers can create both long lasting and soluble items. For example, 3-D printing can be used to "print" pills that contain multiple drugs, which will help patients with the organisation, timing and monitoring of multiple medications. This is a true example of technology and medicine working together.

## Artificial Organs

To take 3D printing up another notch, bio-printing is also an emerging medical technology. While it was initially ground-breaking to be able to regenerate skin cells for skin draughts for burn victims, this has slowly given way to even more exciting possibilities. Scientist have been able to create blood vessels, synthetic ovaries and even a pancreas. These artificial organs then grow within the patient's body to replace original faulty one. The ability to supply artificial organs that are not rejected by the body's immune system could be revolutionary, saving millions of patients that depend on life-saving transplants every year.

## Health Wearables

The demand for wearable devices has grown since their introduction in the past few years, since the release of bluetooth in 2000. People today use their phone to track everything from their steps, physical fitness and heartbeat, to their sleeping patterns. The advancement of these wearable technologies is in conjunction with rising chronic diseases like diabetes and cardiovascular disease, and aim to combat these by helping patients to monitor and improve their fitness.

In late 2018, Apple made headlines with their ground breaking Apple Series 4 Watch that has an integrated ECG to monitor the wearer's heart rhythms. Within days of its release, customers were raving about the life saving technology, which is able to detect potentially dangerous heart conditions much earlier than usual. The wearable devices market is forecast to reach $67 billion by 2024.

## Precision Medicine

As medical technology advances it is becoming more and more personalised to individual patients. Precision medicine, for example, allows physicians to select medicines and therapies to treat diseases, such as cancer, based on an individual's genetic make-up. This personalised medicine is far more effective than other types of treatment as it attacks tumours based on the patient's specific genes and proteins, causing gene mutations and making it more easily destroyed by the cancer meds.

Precision medicine can also be used to treat rheumatoid arthritis. It uses a similar mechanism of attacking the disease's vulnerable genes to weaken it and reduce symptoms and joint damage.

## Virtual Reality

Virtual reality has been around for some time. However, recently, with medical and technological advances, medical students have been able to get close to real life experience using technology. Sophisticated tools help them gain the experience they need by rehearsing procedures and providing a visual understanding of how the human anatomy is connected. The VR devices will also serve as a great aid for patients, helping with diagnosis, treatment plans and to help prepare them for procedures they are facing. It has also proved very useful in patient rehabilitation and recovery.

## Telehealth

In a technologically driven world, it's thought that as many as 60% of customers prefer digitally-led services. Telehealth describes a quickly developing technology that allows patients to receive medical care through their digital devices, instead of waiting for face-to-face appointments with their doctor. For example, highly-personalised mobile apps are being developed which allow patients to speak virtually with physicians and other medical professionals to receive instant diagnosis and medical advice.

With oversubscribed services, telehealth gives patients different access points to healthcare when and where they need it. It is particularly useful for patients managing chronic conditions as it provides them with consistent, convenient and cost-effective care. The global telemedicine market is expected to be worth $113.1 billion by 2025.

## CRISPR

Clustered Regularly Interspaced Short Palindromic Repeats (CRISPR) is the most advanced gene-editing technology yet. It works by harnessing the natural mechanisms of the immune systems of bacterium cells of invading viruses, which is then able to "cut out" infected DNA strands. This cutting of DNA is what has the power to potentially transform the way we treat disease. By modifying genes, some of the biggest threats to our health, like cancer and HIV, could potentially be overcome in a matter of years.

However, as with all powerful tools there are several controversies surrounding its widespread use, mostly over humanity's right to "play God" and worries over gene-editing being used to produce hordes of designer babies. CRISPR is still a first-generation tool and its full capabilities are not yet understood.

As the years pass, technology in pharmaceuticals and medicine will continue to improve. People are living longer and fewer diseases are deemed incurable. Jobs in the pharmaceutical industry are in higher demand now than ever. Who knows what the next year will bring in medical advancements!

# Stem Cells Have Changed Everything, but Stem Cell Research Was Hindered by Research Bans

*Michael White*

*Michael White is an assistant professor of genetics at the Washington University School of Medicine in St. Louis, where he is a member of the Center for Genome Sciences and Systems Biology. He is a cofounder of the online science public house and blog* The Finch and Pea.

E mbryonic stem cell research is at the leading edge of a series of moral hazards," declared George W. Bush in August 2001, as he announced his administration's new policy restricting federal funds for biomedical research involving human embryonic stem cells. The moral hazards Bush referred to defined a conflict between medical research and pro-life politics: Scientists and patients hoped that embryonic stem cells, with their unique capacity to develop into any type of cell in the body, would lead to radical new treatments for presently incurable diseases, while pro-life organizations opposed the destruction of human embryos necessary to obtain stem cells. As Bush put it, the issue "juxtapos[es] the need to protect life in all its phases with the prospect of saving and improving life in all its stages."

The conflict over stem cells soon became a high-profile political controversy with real consequences: It shifted political control of the United States Senate to the Democrats in 2006 and led California to create a new $3 billion stem cell research initiative, despite opposition from the Catholic Church and a coalition of pro-life organizations. Less than two months after Barack Obama took office, he eliminated Bush's restrictions with an executive order pointedly titled "Removing Barriers to Responsible Scientific

"How Scientific Progress Is Changing the Stem Cell Debate," by Michael White, the Social Justice Foundation, August 28, 2015. Reprinted by permission.

Research Involving Human Stem Cells." In recent years, the controversy over stem cells has waned somewhat, but it hasn't gone fully away: In its current party platform, the GOP opposes any stem cell research that involves "the destruction of embryonic human life."

While the moral conflict over embryonic stem cells is unlikely to be resolved by compromise, recent technological progress may soon render the controversy largely moot. After a decade-long series of discoveries, two new studies describe developments that will likely enable medical researchers to skip the stem cells in medical treatments that were once thought to be impossible without them.

To see why avoiding embryonic stem cells is a big advance, it's important to understand why researchers and patients placed so much hope in them in the first place. In essence, embryonic stem cells seemed to offer a unique source of biological replacement parts, creating an opportunity to treat difficult diseases in a radically new way. Many chronic, incurable diseases are caused by the progressive loss of critical cells that are not re-generated in the sick person's body, such as dopamine-secreting neurons in Parkinson's or insulin-producing pancreatic cells in diabetes. Drugs can treat symptoms or slow the progression of such diseases, but they can't restore lost or damaged cells—this is why these diseases are incurable.

In contrast to drugs, embryonic stem cells actually offer a cure. Because they have the capacity to become any cell type in the body, they can be used to derive replacements for a patient's lost or damaged cells. By transplanting these replacement cells into patients, medical researchers could reverse the otherwise irreversible symptoms of the disease. If successful, the results would be transformative: Parkinson's patients would regain control of their movements, diabetics could stop taking insulin, and patients suffering from macular degeneration would regain their vision. In 2001, embryonic stem cell-based therapies were completely hypothetical, though similar ones using more limited, non-embryonic stem cells—such as bone marrow transplants, which transfer specialized blood stem cells to treat leukemia—had existed for decades. Today, these embryonic stem cell treatments have been shown to work in laboratory mice but not much more; however, the first human clinical trials for a embryonic stem cell therapy for macular degeneration are now underway.

A big scientific question that has haunted the embryonic stem cell debate is this: Are these cells the only option? If therapeutic replacement cells could be obtained without using embryos, the controversy would end. And there has long been a good reason to believe that an alternative source of cells might be possible. Because nearly every cell in our bodies carries exactly the same genetic information, any cell—not just embryonic stem cells—could theoretically be converted into any other type of cell. A meter-long motor neuron that conducts electrical signals down the spine is physically and functionally very different from the micron-scale hepatocytes that metabolize carbs in the liver. Yet the neuron carries the same genes as the hepatocyte; the reason they differ is because the neuron has switched on a different set of genes. By finding a way to convert an ethically non-controversial source of cells—such as skin cells—into the cell types needed for therapies, we could end the debate.

But turning on genes to formulate a specialized cell is a complicated process involving a series of steps in which genes are switched on and off in a certain sequence. Embryonic stem cells lie at the beginning of this series; they are the crossroads from which one of many different paths can be chosen, leading to a final, specialized cell type. For a long time, researchers believed that cells travel these paths in only one direction: Once cells reach their final state, they almost never leave it. And though a neuron and a liver cell may have exactly the same genes, scientists believed they couldn't change one into the other—as they say in Maine, you can't get there from here. There is no shortcut from a neuron to a liver cell; you have to start with a stem cell.

While this idea is true inside our bodies, researchers have now demonstrated that it is not this way in a test tube. In Nobel Prize-winning work published in 2006 and 2007, Japanese researcher Shinya Yamanaka and his colleagues managed to reset skin cells to a stem cell state, creating what are called "induced pluripotent stem cells," and thus demonstrating how to get stem cells without using embryos. Induced stem cells have been an enormous boon to disease research, but they currently can't be used in stem cell transplant therapies because they usually contain mutations that would put patients at risk for developing tumors.

More recently, scientists discovered that there are, in fact, shortcuts between different types of cells. In 2010, a team at Stanford converted mouse skin cells directly into neurons, without creating stem cells first. And just last year, a team of Chinese scientists converted human skin cells into liver cells, which functioned normally when transplanted into mice. However, as with the creation of induced pluripotent stem cells, these studies relied on genetic manipulations that make the resulting cells inappropriate for therapies.

But in a pair of studies published earlier this month, two teams of Chinese researchers have demonstrated how to re-program skin cells into neurons without using genetic modifications, opening up a major new pathway for cell therapies that don't require human embryos. In each case, the researchers devised a drug cocktail that caused skin cells to shut off one set of genes and turn on another. Importantly, this process happens without any permanent changes to the cells' DNA—the drug cocktail simply prompts the skin cells to activate dormant neuronal genes, causing them to transform into neurons. In one study, researchers found that a combination of four drugs was enough to re-program mouse skin cells into functional neurons. In the second study, another research team achieved a similar result with human skin cells, using a different chemical cocktail. This latter team then went one step further: They took skin cells from an Alzheimer's patient and re-programmed those into neurons. The resulting neurons had some of the protein build-up that is characteristic of Alzheimer's disease, demonstrating that this method of re-programming cells—in addition to its possible therapeutic value for patients—is a potentially powerful way to study a disease in a petri dish.

Results like these have the potential to settle the debate over embryonic stem cells. The controversy isn't over quite yet though—while the newer techniques are immediately useful in research, they have yet to yield any therapies. And because embryonic stem cells are useful for studying how different types of cells develop naturally in the body, they still play an important role in ongoing biomedical research. However, viable alternatives to embryonic stem cells—which were only a hope in 2001—are now a reality. Technological progress has a well-known tendency to create moral controversies, something that was certainly true when scientists first learned how to derive stem cells from embryos. But in this case, technology will likely help us settle the controversy as well.

# The Drug Approval Process Is Confusing

*Comment Central*

*Launched in 2016, Comment Central is a platform for policy debate and discussion. With an editorially hands-off attitude, the website features news and opinion from a range of perspectives.*

Recent scientific studies suggest we are making progress in the treatment of Alzheimer's and other deadly diseases. However, a burdensome and costly regulatory system is needlessly prolonging our progress.

Pharmaceutical medicine has had a profound impact on our modern human history. More progress has been made in advancing our understanding of human medicine over the past century than all the previous centuries combined. Smallpox, polio and leprosy—once intractable human diseases, indiscriminate of wealth, race or social class, are now being consigned to the annals of history. The discovery of antibiotics has rendered many deadly bacterial infections virtually innocuous. The 1950s saw the introduction of Chlorpromazine—the world's first antipsychotic medication—paving the way for the transformation and closure of the macabre Victorian asylums.

But as one war is won another begins. The startling rate of medical advancement has brought with it new challenges. As life expectancy increases, so too has the prevalence of other diseases such as cancer and neurodegenerative disorders, like dementia.

The explosion in new and effective treatments for once deadly diseases has been checked by a similar growth in red-tape and regulation, inhibiting patients' access to lifesaving medication.

The onerous process costs time, money and lives. In the US—the world leader in the development of new pharmaceutical drugs—the cost of delivering a drug from "bench to bedside" has increased

"Drug Approval Gives Me a Headache," *Comment Central*, September 7, 2018. Reprinted by permission.

exponentially since the 1970s. A US study by the Tufts Center for Drug Development found that in 1975 for a new drug to be approved the pharmaceutical industry spent on average the equivalent of £65 million in today's prices for research and development costs. By 1987, that figure had tripled, to £195 million, and by 2005 costs had soared to £800 million. Cancer Research UK now estimates the figure to be approximately £1.1 billion.

The Tufts study also investigated the driving forces behind these soaring costs. Onerous requirements for supplemental testing, even when a drug has not been shown to pose any health risks, as well as costly delays triggered by unjustified demands for additional data were key factors. It found that from 1999 to 2005 the average length of a clinical trial increased by 70 per cent; the average number of routine procedures per trial increased by 65 per cent; and the average clinical trial staff work burden increased by 67 per cent.

This symptom is not exclusive to America. In the UK, the European Medicines Agency (EMA)—a key arbiter in deciding whether new drugs enter the British market—is responsible for even more pronounced delays.

Even if a drug is approved in one jurisdiction, such as the US, it is often subject to supplementary testing requirements here in the UK & Europe, and vice-versa.

These soaring costs are stifling innovation and delaying the arrival of new life-saving drugs. Analysis by the global consulting firm, Deloitte, suggests the result is that drug companies are becoming more cautious and less innovative in their approach. An increasing number of new drug submissions are for "me too" drugs—drugs that are structurally very similar to already known drugs, with only minor differences. In the US, between 2006 and 2011, only ten truly innovative treatments were approved by the FDA out of a total of 35 submissions. The majority of new molecules launched between 2007 and 2011 already had established mechanisms of action.

The rising approval costs are also impacting on patients in other ways. In a bid to recoup the increasing costs incurred, pharmaceutical companies increase their prices, often at levels that preclude the ability for Government regulators, such as NICE—with their antiquated approval processes—to grant marketing licences to public health providers, including the NHS.

Despite international efforts to streamline approval processes, the systems remain cumbersome. In the UK, the Early Access to Medicines Scheme (EAMS) has been established allowing patients with life-threatening illnesses to access unapproved medicines. Similar programmes have been established in other jurisdictions. But these are sticking plaster solutions that fail to adequately address the problem. More needs to be done.

It is vital the various jurisdictional regulators collaborate more closely to improve their approval procedures. In the UK, the main organisation tasked with reviewing drug safety, the Medicines & Healthcare products Regulatory Agency (MHRA), should be encouraged to work more closely with the US Food and Drug Administration (USFDA) and the EMA to streamline and standardise testing protocols. If successfully achieved, the economic and healthcare benefits would be immeasurable.

The Australian government has announced the introduction of a novel solution to help facilitate new drug development and delivery. Under the new approval process, any drug that has been listed by a comparable overseas regulator, including the US Food and Drug Administration and the European Medicines Agency, can now be fast-tracked for approval and sale in Australia. This will remove superfluous regulation, lower drug company costs, encourage innovation and afford Australian patients quicker access to new medicines.

Opponents of simplifying existing drug approval processes are understandably haunted by the devastating impact of Thalidomide. Developed, approved and distributed to patients in West Germany during the 1950s at a time when effective drug trialling was in its infancy, the drug soon spread in popularity and was introduced to other jurisdictions (although notably in the US the FDA rejected the drug on the grounds of safety concerns). Had drug trialling and distribution in 1950s been subject to the same standards as those present in the 1970s, the side effects of the drug would have been identified and authorisation for the treatment of morning sickness rejected.

Today, following further research, and with a fuller understanding of the drug's side-effect profile, prescribed in the appropriate settings, Thalidomide is an important weapon in the battle against multiple myeloma.

Better regulation does work. In 1987, in the midst of the HIV/AIDS pandemic—and motivated by onerous approval requirements for promising investigational drugs—AIDS Coalition to Unleash Power (ACT UP) was formed. Through a combination of civil disobedience, effective lobbying and peaceful protest, the group successfully saw Congress approve the accelerated approval pathway for HIV medication. The result was the faster introduction of effective anti-retroviral therapies. Today, HIV has been transformed from what was once a death sentence into a chronic condition.

Effective drug trialling is a vital component to ensuring public health, while ensuring public confidence in pharmaceuticals. But too much regulation, although harder to see, can be far more deadly and detrimental to patient lives.

# Government Regulation Adds Costs and Red Tape, Weighing Down Scientific Innovation

*Dean Baker*

*Dean Baker cofounded the Center for Economic and Policy Research in 1999. His areas of research include housing and macroeconomics, intellectual property, Social Security, Medicare, and European labor markets. He is the author of several books, including* Rigged: How Globalization and the Rules of the Modern Economy Were Structured to Make the Rich Richer.

I often begin talks by telling my audience that "drugs are cheap." This typically leads people to believe they are listening to a crazy person. At least in the United States, everyone knows that drugs are not cheap. It is common for prescriptions of brand drugs to cost several hundred dollars. More expensive drugs can easily cost tens of thousands of dollars a year. And, the new generation of cancer drugs carry list prices that run into the hundreds of thousands of dollars a year.

If people are lucky enough to have good insurance, most of the cost will be picked up by the insurance company, but insurers are not happy paying tens of thousands of dollars a year for a patient's drugs either. To save money and discourage usage insurers are increasingly requiring substantial copayments. These copayments can be a huge blow to patients who may already not be able to hold down a full-time job because of their health. Paying 25 percent of the bill for a drug selling for $40,000 a year, still comes to $10,000 a year. That's close to 20 percent of the median family income in the United States.

This is a background that is familiar to people in the United States who have someone with a serious health condition among their family or friends. They know drugs are extremely expensive for them. But, I am not crazy for saying that drugs are cheap. They are in fact in almost all cases cheap to manufacture.

To take one example that has frequently been in the news in the United States, the Hepatitis C drug Sovaldi has a list price of $84,000 for a three-month course of treatment. By all accounts, the drug is genuine breakthrough in the treatment of the Hepatitis C, in most cases curing a debilitating and sometimes fatal disease. There has been an extensive public debate as to whether insurers or government health care programs should be forced to pay for this expensive drug. The issue is complicated further by the fact that many people suffering from Hepatitis C might have contracted it through intravenous drug use.

The United States is estimated to have 3 million people suffering from Hepatitis C. This implies a bill of well over one hundred billion dollars if everyone were to be treated, even if its manufacturer, Gilead Sciences, provided substantial discounts.

But it doesn't cost $84,000 or anything close to that figure to manufacture Sovaldi. In fact, in India a high quality generic version of the drug is available for $200 for a three month course of treatment, less than 0.3 percent of the list price in the United States. We wouldn't need a major debate to decide whether we would spend $200 for a drug that would hugely improve a patient's health and would possibly save their life. The reason we have this debate is that the drug has a list price that is more than 400 times higher.

## Patent Monopolies: The Villain Behind High Prices

Of course people have realized at this point that the reason Sovaldi has a high price in the United States is that Gilead Sciences has a patent monopoly on the drug. This monopoly gives it the exclusive right to sell the drug in the United States. The US government will arrest anyone who tries to sell Sovaldi in competition with Gilead Sciences. The United States is unique in that we both grant pharmaceutical companies a patent monopoly on their drugs, and then let them sell the drugs for whatever price they want. Other wealthy countries also grant patent monopolies, which are required by a number of international agreements, but they have some form of price control which limits what companies can charge. For this reason, drug prices in other wealthy countries are typically around half of the price in the United States.

My comments will refer largely to the United States. This is first and foremost because it is the market with which I am most familiar. However the same problems appear in other countries, even if they may not be as extreme as in the United States. Furthermore, it is the explicit goal of the United States government to use trade agreements like the Trans-Atlantic Trade and Investment Pact to raise the price of drugs in other countries to US levels. So the United States may well represent the future for the prescription drug market in Sweden and the rest of Europe.

## Patent Monopolies as Incentive for Innovation

The rationale for patent monopolies is to provide an incentive for drug companies to innovate. It is expensive to develop new drugs. Even if the industry has a tendency to exaggerate the cost, and downplay the extent to which they benefit from publicly financed research, they do encounter substantial expenses that they would not be able to recover if new drugs were sold in a free market. The question for critics of this system is whether there are feasible alternatives to patent monopolies that would be as effective in producing new drugs and would be less wasteful than the patent system. While we will not know the answer to this question until we actually have an alternative in place to provide a basis for comparison, there are strong reasons for believing that an alternative system would be vastly more efficient. In addition, a system in which drugs were sold at their free market price would forever end the situation where people are unable to afford drugs that are essential for their life or health.

## Problems of Patent Monopolies

There are two distinct types of problems associated with patent monopolies. The first stems simply from the fact that the patent protected price makes drugs much more expensive for patients than the free market price. As a result, fewer patients have access to drugs they need and/or they have to go through more obstacles to gain access. The other set of problems stem from the behavior of drug companies to maximize their profits. This is often referred to as "rent-seeking" behavior. It amounts to actions by drug companies which serve no productive use from an economic standpoint. Rent-seeking behavior is exclusively redistributive. It allows drug companies to increase their profits at the expense of patients, insurers and governments.

It is worth noting that these points are completely standard in economic analyses of trade. If someone were to propose a 20 percent tariff on imported steel, any serious economist could quickly point out the loss to consumers as a result of this arbitrary increase in the price of steel. They would also point to rent-seeking activities by the steel companies, for example lobbying politicians to extend and increase the tariff, as a further source of waste. The same logic would apply to patent protection for prescription drugs, except the price increases are equivalent to tariffs of 1000 percent or even 10,000 percent of the free market price. Unfortunately economists spend far more time worrying about the costs associated with 20 percent tariffs on things like steel than they do on patent monopolies for prescription drugs.

The first type of loss, from people having to pay high prices, takes several different forms. The most obvious is the case where people simply can't buy the drug because patent monopolies raise the price by several thousand percent above the free market price. The result is that people get worse health care and quite possibly die. But even those who might be able to afford the drug often suffer because of the high price. In the United States it is common for many lower income people to cut pills in half or to take them every other day in order to make a prescription go further. In many cases this can seriously undermine the effectiveness of the drug.

Even when people have reasonably good insurance they often have to battle their insurer to pay the cost of an expensive drug. This may mean that they have to go to a second physician to verify that an expensive drug is in fact necessary. In some cases an insurer has a policy where they will pay for a drug for a particular use, but not for the use prescribed by the doctor. This can lead doctors to put down a false diagnosis so that their patient is able to have their drug covered by the insurance company. Needless to say, this can create a problem for a patient in future treatment since it means they will have an inaccurate medical record.

There is also a massive gaming process whereby the drug companies try to get around insurers' efforts to discourage the use of an expensive drug. Sometimes the pharmaceutical company will provide coupons to cover patients' copayment, making them more likely to opt for an expensive drug and leave the insurers with the bill. When its patent on the allergy drug Claritin expired, Schering-Plough pushed to make it an over-the-counter drug not requiring a prescription. Since insurance generally doesn't cover the cost of over-the-counter drugs, this action meant that the generic versions of Claritin would likely cost patients more money than their co-pay on Schering-Plough's new patented product, Clarinex.

In addition to this gaming, the high price of patent protected drugs has created a whole industry of "pharmacy benefit managers" who act as intermediaries between insurers or hospitals and drug companies. They negotiate prices that typically are substantial discounts from the list prices, leaving the uninsured as the only ones who might actually pay the full list price. In any case, there would be no reason for the industry of pharmacy benefit managers to exist if prescription drugs were sold in a free market.

## Costs on the Research Side Due to Rent-Seeking

Science advances most quickly when the research is fully open. In this situation, the community of researchers can assess research and look for flaws and also quickly build upon interesting findings. Openness has no place in research supported by patent monopolies. It is in the interest of the pharmaceutical company to make available only the information needed to receive a patent. The test results it submits to the Food and Drug Administration (FDA) are kept secret from the public, with firms only disclosing the findings they choose to share. Needless to say, these results are likely to be ones that reflect well on their drugs, with the companies less likely to highlight results that question a drug's effectiveness or suggest it could be harmful.

This was the allegation in the case of the arthritis drug Vioxx, where the manufacturer allegedly concealed evidence the drug increased the risk of heart attack and stroke among patients with heart conditions. The result was a number of strokes and heart attacks that might have been prevented if doctors and patients knew of the risks associated with Vioxx. Drug companies also have an incentive to promote the use of their drug in situations where it may not be appropriate. Efforts to promote drugs for "off-label" use are a regular source of scandal in the business press.

A recent analysis that looked at five prominent instances in which it was alleged that either drug companies concealed information about their drugs or marketed them for inappropriate uses, found that the cost born by patients was in the range of $27 billion annually over the years 1994–2008. While this estimate is far from precise, it suggests that the cost associated with improper drug use due to deliberate misrepresentations and mis-marketing is substantial, quite likely in the range of the amount spent by the industry on drug research. Also, it is worth repeating that these costs, in terms of bad health outcomes, are the result of deliberate actions stemming from the perverse incentives created by patent monopolies, not costs from the sort of mistakes that are an inevitable part of the research process.

Patent monopolies also distort the research process itself. Most obviously they encourage drug companies to pursue patent rents rather than finding drugs that meet the most urgent health needs.

This means that if a pharmaceutical company produces a drug for a particular condition that earns large amounts of revenue, its competitors have a strong incentive to try to produce similar drugs for the same condition to capture a share of the rents.

For example, in the case of Sovaldi, Merck and AbbVie, along with several smaller drug manufacturers, are rushing to market alternatives to Sovaldi as treatments for Hepatitis C. In a context where Gilead Sciences, the maker of Sovaldi, has a monopoly on effective treatments for Hepatitis C, this sort of competition is highly desirable because it will lead to lower prices. However, if Sovaldi was being sold in a free market at $200 to $300 for a course of treatment, there would be little reason to waste the time of highly skilled scientists finding additional treatments for a condition where an effective drug already exists. If drugs were sold without patent protection, research dollars would usually be better devoted to developing a drug for a condition where no effective treatment exists than developing duplicative drugs for a condition that can be well-treated by an existing drug.

Patent protection also is likely to slow and/or distort the research process by encouraging secrecy. Research advances most quickly when it is open. However, companies seeking profits through patent monopolies have incentive to disclose as little information as possible in order to avoid helping competitors. This forces researchers to work around rather than build upon research findings. Williams (2010) found that the patenting of DNA sequences in the human genome project slowed future innovation and product development by between 20 to 30 percent.

Finally, relying on patent incentives to support medical research encourages drug companies to direct research toward finding a patentable product. This means that if evidence suggests that a condition can be most effectively treated through diet, exercise, environmental factors, or even old off-patent drugs, a pharmaceutical manufacturer would have no incentive to pursue this research. Ideally, the manufacturer would make this evidence publicly available so that researchers supported by the government, universities, or other non-profit organizations could pursue it, but there is little incentive for them to go this route. In fact, if they are concerned that such research could lead to an alternative to a patentable product that they might develop or be in the process of developing, their incentive is to conceal the research.

## Lawyering and Lobbying: Other Forms of Patent-Induced Waste

When the government is the payer, which is to some extent the case in the US, the willingness to pay for a particular drug can often be the outcome of a political battle, with the drug's producer working with patients to pressure the government to pay for drugs of questionable value. While the government in the U.S. plays a smaller role in providing health care than in most other wealthy countries, it nonetheless plays a huge role in shaping the market. It directly pays for drugs through Medicare, Medicaid, and other government health care programs, and can set standards that effectively require private insurers to pay for drugs. This gives the pharmaceutical industry a substantial incentive to be involved in the political process. According to Center for Responsive Politics, the pharmaceutical industry ranked 5th in campaign contributions to members of Congress in 2016. The broader category of health related industries ranked second, behind only finance, insurance, and real estate in total contributions to politicians.

Because this involves decisions on public health, the victory of drug companies is not just a question of getting more money at the expense of competitors or the general public. They may lobby for policies that are detrimental to public health in order to boost their profits. For example, pharmaceutical companies that produce pain relief medication have been leading the fight against medical marijuana. It turns out that marijuana is an effective substitute in many cases for prescription pain medications. In order to protect its market share, the industry is trying to keep a major potential competitor off the market. There can be major consequences for public health as patients take stronger and more addictive medications when marijuana may be an effective treatment. Similarly, the industry uses its ties to disease groups to try to keep generic competitors from being covered by the government or insurers. This is precisely the sort of corruption that would be expected in a situation where there is such a huge gap between the monopoly price and the cost of production.

The fact that there is so much money as stake with patent protection in pharmaceuticals means that the sector is also a primary target for litigation. Pharmaceutical companies routinely bring suits to harass competitors, discourage generic competition, or to gain a slice of the patent rents associated with a highly profitable drug. The pharmaceutical and medical equipment industries together accounted for almost a quarter of the patent-related lawsuits over the years 1995–2014. The suits in the pharmaceutical sector also had the highest median damage settlement, with medical equipment coming in a close third just behind the telecommunication industry.

In any legal battle, there is a fundamental asymmetry between the situation of brand drug manufacturers, which have the right to sell a drug at monopoly prices for the duration of its patent protection, and potential generic entrants, who are looking to have the right to sell a drug in a competitive market. This means that the brand manufacturer stands much more to lose than the generic producer stands to gain. As a result, the brand producer has an incentive to spend much more on legal expenses than a potential generic competitor if doing so can block, or at least delay, generic competition. The brand producer also may attempt side payments as a way to discourage the entry by a generic competitor. While this collusion is illegal, it can be hard to detect, especially if the payment takes the form of a contract (e.g. the generic producer is paid to manufacture one of the brand manufacturer's drugs) which could have been reached without any collusion.

For all of the reasons discussed above, patent-supported research is particularly ill-suited for the pharmaceutical sector.

The question is whether it is possible to design an alternative mechanism that can be equally effective in developing new drugs.

## Publicly Financed Pharmaceutical Research

The basic logic of a system of publicly financed medical research would be that the government expand its current funding for biomedical research, which now goes primarily through NIH, by an amount that is roughly equal to the patent supported research currently being conducted by the pharmaceutical industry. Pharma, the industry trade group, puts this funding level at roughly $50 billion or 0.3 percent of GDP, a figure that is also consistent with data from the National Science Foundation. That would be a reasonable target, with the idea that the public funding would eventually replace the patent-supported funding. Adding in research on medical equipment and tests would increase this figure by $12–15 billion.

In order to minimize the risk of political interference and also the risk that excessive bureaucracy could impede innovation, it would be desirable that the bulk of this funding would be committed to private firms under long-term contracts (e.g. 10–15 years). This would allow for the imposition of clear rules that apply to all research directly or indirectly funded by the public sector, without a need for micro-management. The contracts would be subject to regular oversight for their duration, but the contractors would be free to set priorities for which lines of research to support. The contractors could also freely subcontract, just as the major pharmaceutical companies do now. They could also use their funds to buy research produced by other companies, just as the pharmaceutical industry does at present. As the period for a contract approached its end, the contractor could attempt to gain a new long-term contract. It would argue its case based on its track record with the prior contract.

The basic rules governing these contracts would be that all the results stemming from publicly financed research would be placed in the public domain, subject to copyleft-type restrictions. This means that any patents for drugs, research tools, or other intermediate steps developed by contractors or subcontractors, would be freely available for anyone to use, subject to the condition that they also would place any subsequent patents in the public domain. Similarly, test results used to get approval for a drug from Food and Drug Administration would be available for any generic producer to use to gain acceptance for their own product.

In addition to requiring that patents be placed in the public domain, there would also be a requirement that all research findings be made available to the public as quickly as practical. This means, for example, that results from pre-clinical testing be made available as soon as they are known, so that other researchers could benefit from the findings. This should prevent unnecessary duplication and allow for more rapid progress in research. These restrictions would apply to both direct contractors and any sub-contractors that were hired.

This disclosure requirement would not be a negative for participants in the context of this sort of open-source contract system. Because the goal is to generate useful innovations rather than procure a patent, a contractor would be able to make an effective case for the usefulness of their work even if competitors were the ones that ultimately used it to develop a useful drug or medical device. The incentive in this system is to disseminate any interesting findings as widely as possible in the hope that other researchers will be able to build upon them.

The contracting system in the Defense Department can be seen as a loose model for contracting in pharmaceutical research. When the Defense Department is planning a major project, such as a new fighter plane or submarine, it will typically sign a contract with a major corporation like General Electric or Lockheed. The contractor will generally subcontract much of the project, because it is not prepared to do all the work in-house. The same would be the case with a contractor doing research developing pharmaceuticals or medical equipment, although the expected results will be somewhat less clearly specified. While that is a disadvantage of contracting with medical research, because the outcomes will be less well-defined, a major advantage is that there would be no excuse for secrecy in the medical research process. There is a clear justification for secrecy in military research, because it wouldn't make sense to allow potential enemies to have access to the latest military technology. By contrast, biomedical research will be advanced more quickly by allowing the greatest possible access.

Secrecy has often been an important factor allowing military contractors to conceal waste or fraud, because only a very select group of people have access to the specific terms of a contract and the nature of the work a company is doing. In the case of biomedical research, there is no reason that the terms of the contract would not be fully public. And, all research findings would have to be posted in a timely manner. With such rules, it should be possible to quickly identify any contractor whose output clearly did not correspond to the money they were receiving from the government. For all the instances of waste and fraud in military contracting, it nonetheless has been effective in giving the US the most technologically advanced military in the world.

Because the system of patent protection and rules on data exclusivity is now enshrined in a large number of international agreements that would be difficult to circumvent, it is important that an alternative system work around this structure. As proposed here, patent protection under current rules would still be available to drug companies conducting research with their own funds. However, they would run the risk that at the point where they have an FDA-approved drug, there is a new drug available at generic prices that is comparably effective. This sort of competition would likely force the company to sell its drug at a price comparable to the generic, leaving it little margin for recouping its research costs.

Simply the risk of this sort of generic competition should make the current system of patent-financed drug development unprofitable, especially if the industry's claims about its research costs are anywhere close to being accurate. In this way, the existing rules on patents can be left in place, even as a new system of publicly financed research comes to dominate the process of drug development.

[…]

## Publicly Funded Clinical Trials

Switching all at once to a system of fully funded research would likely be a difficult step both politically and practically. This would involve a radical transformation of a massive industry of a sort that is rarely seen in the US or anywhere else. Fortunately, there is an intermediate step that can be used to advance toward a system of fully funded research which would offer enormous benefits in its own right.

There is a simple and basic divide in the research process between the pre-clinical phase of drug development and the clinical phase. The pre-clinical phase involves the development of new drugs or new uses of existing drugs and preliminary tests on lab animals. The clinical phase involves testing on humans and eventually proceeding to the FDA approval process if the earlier phases of testing are successful. The clinical testing phase accounts for more than 60 percent of spending on research, although this number is reduced if a return is imputed on the pre-clinical testing phase, because there is a considerably longer lag between pre-clinical expenditures and an approved drug than with clinical tests.

The clinical testing process involves a standard set of procedures, and is therefore far more routinized than the pre-clinical portion of drug development. For this reason, the clinical testing portion of the drug development process could be more easily adapted to a program of direct public funding. The model could be the same as discussed earlier, with the government contracting on a long-term basis with existing or new drug companies. However, the contracts would specify the testing of drugs in particular areas. As was the case described earlier, all results would be fully public, and all patent and related rights associated with the testing process would be put in the public domain subject to copyleft-type rules. This would likely mean that in many cases the contracting companies would have to buy up rights to a compound(s) before they initiated testing, because another company held a patent on it.

There are many advantages to separating out the clinical testing portion of drug development rather than attempting to fully replace patent supported research all at once. First, it would be much easier to slice off particular areas to experiment with public funding. For example, it should be possible to set aside a certain amount of funding for clinical trials for new cancer or heart drugs without worrying about fully replacing private support for research in these areas. Also, it should be possible to obtain dividends much more quickly in the form of new drugs being available at generic prices. The time lag between the beginning of preclinical research and an approved drug can be as long as 20 years. The clinical testing process typically takes less than eight years and can be considerably shorter if a drug's benefits become quickly evident in trials.

Another important early dividend from the public funding of clinical trials is that the results of these trials would be posted as soon as they are available. This means that researchers and doctors would not only have access to the summary statistics showing the success rates in the treatment group relative to the control group, but they would also have access to the data on specific individuals in the trial. This would allow them to independently analyze the data to determine if there were differences in outcomes based on age, gender, or other factors. It would also allow for researchers to determine the extent to which interactions with other drugs affected the effectiveness of a new drug.

In addition, the public disclosure of test results may put pressure on the pharmaceutical industry to change its practices. The problem of misreporting or concealing results in order to promote a drug is one that arises in the process of clinical testing. While misrepresented results can be a problem at any stage in the drug development process, misrepresentations at the pre-clinical phase are unlikely to have health consequences because they will be uncovered in clinical testing. The problem of patients being prescribed drugs that are less effective than claimed or possible harmful to certain patients due to misrepresentations is entirely an issue with clinical testing. If experiments with a limited number of publicly funded clinical trials can change the norms on disclosure of test results, they will have made an enormous contribution to public health.

## Conclusion

The system of relying on patent monopolies for financing prescription drug research has enormous costs. These costs take exactly the form economists predict from a government intervention in the market. The main difference with patent monopolies on drugs is that the intervention is far larger than most other forms of intervention that arise in policy debates like tariffs on trade or various excise taxes and subsidies. Furthermore, since drugs are often essential for people's lives and health, the costs take a different form than paying higher prices for items like shoes or furniture. These costs are likely to rise in the years ahead as the gap between the patent-protected prices and free market prices grow ever larger.

For this reason, we should be considering alternative mechanisms for supporting prescription drug research. I have argued that a system of direct government funding, which relies on private companies working on long-term contracts, is likely to be far more efficient than the current system. By paying all research costs upfront, drugs could be sold at free market prices without monopoly protections, just like most other products. Also, since a condition of receiving public money is that all findings would be fully public as soon as is practical, doctors will be able to make more informed decisions in prescribing drugs. In addition, research is likely to advance more quickly in a context of openness than secrecy.

For these reasons, we should be looking for alternatives to patent-financed drug research. There is much room for improvement.

CHAPTER 3

# Does Current Regulation of Illicit Drugs Inhibit Medical Innovation?

# Research in Drug Innovation May Not Be Aimed in the Right Direction

*Christopher-Paul Milne and Kenneth I. Kaitin*

*Dr. Christopher-Paul Milne joined the Center for the Study of Drug Development at the Tufts University School of Medicine (Tufts CSDD) in Boston over twenty years ago as a senior research fellow. He has published extensively on market access factors, incentive programs for studies, and tracking the progress of regulatory and research initiatives. Dr. Kenneth Kaitin is a professor at Tufts University School of Medicine and the Director of the Tufts Center for the Study of Drug Development. He is also an internationally recognized expert in drug development science and policy.*

A host of challenges confront healthcare authorities worldwide. Topping the list is the demand for innovative new medicines to treat a range of both infectious and non-communicable diseases, while containing spiraling healthcare costs. The challenge is particularly great in therapeutic areas where, despite significant medical need and economic impact, the technical challenges and commercial risk of development serve as disincentives to drug sponsors. These areas include cardiovascular diseases as well as diseases and disorders of the central nervous system. Currently, the development and approval of new active substances, with its disproportionate focus on oncology, is not in alignment with healthcare needs in most geographic regions. In this article, we discuss the origins of this misalignment and suggest various approaches to address healthcare needs going forward.

"Are Regulation and Innovation Priorities Serving Public Health Needs?" by Christopher-Paul Milne and Kenneth I. Kaitin, Frontiers Media S.A., March 8, 2019. https://www.frontiersin.org/articles/10.3389/fphar.2019.00144/full. Licensed Under CC BY 4.0 International.

## Are New Active Substance Launches Meeting Society's Needs?

Across the globe, spending on medicines as a percentage of overall healthcare expenditures ranges from 5 to 10% in most developed countries to as much as 60% in many emerging economies[1]. Despite the differences, healthcare systems are confronting the same dual challenges of controlling healthcare costs and the critical need for breakthrough treatments. Decision-makers must not only maintain adequate incentives for biomedical innovation, they must also ensure that the new medicines resulting from that innovation are accessible and affordable to patients who need them.

These challenges are increasing in scope and complexity as the world tackles what the World Health Organization (WHO) refers to as the "double burden of disease": i.e., the current crisis of emerging and re-emerging infectious disease epidemics and pandemics, and the growing impact of non-communicable diseases (NCD) on overall mortality and morbidity. Of 56.9 million global deaths in 2016, 40.5 million (71%) were due to NCDs: in particular, cardiovascular (CV) diseases (17.9 million, or 44% of all NCD deaths), cancers [9.0 million (22%)], and respiratory diseases, including asthma and chronic obstructive pulmonary disease [3.8 million (9%)]. Diabetes caused another 1.6 million deaths. Over three-quarters of NCD deaths—31.5 million—occurred in low- and middle-income countries, with about 46% of those deaths occurring in individuals 70 or younger. Currently, healthcare expenditures are an average of 4–5% of GDP in China and India—about half the amount spent in Western Europe and North America. Compounding the challenge is the fact that whereas prescription drugs are often considered one of the most cost-effective forms of medical treatment, the worldwide output of New Active Substances (NAS: the first approval of novel drugs anywhere in the world) has been limited in the range of unmet medical needs being addressed; over the 5-year period 2013–2017, just two therapeutic areas—oncology and infectious diseases—have dominated NAS launches worldwide[2].

## Are Industry Trends Helping or Hurting?

Oncology approvals have become dominant over the last decade. There has also been a surge in approvals in the infectious disease/vaccine (ID) area in recent years, due in part to heightened public awareness of global pandemics and antibiotic resistance. In contrast, approvals of new CV and central nervous system (CNS) agents have fallen far behind, a cause for concern for two reasons. The first is that these trends are not in sync with public healthcare needs. While cancer is certainly a major health issue, it is not the primary health concern in terms of mortality and morbidity; in the US and Western Europe, CV disease (CVD) is number one in overall mortality, and in many emerging and developed markets alike, CVD is associated with growing levels of morbidity and premature death. The second reason for concern is that the NAS approval trends run counter to the mission of national regulatory authorities. These authorities are tasked with addressing medical needs by dedicating energy and resources proportionate to the public health impact of the causative disease. When this is not done, agency decision-making on priorities and resource allocations should be re-evaluated, and recalibrated if necessary.

Current NAS approval trends are troubling in an additional context. While national regulatory authorities influence how many and how fast products reach the marketplace, it is the pharmaceutical industry that typically controls what types of drug candidates enter the development pipeline. The two therapeutic areas that have remained static in recent decades—CNS and CV—represent areas with substantial market potential. Mental health was tied with cancer as one of the four most costly medical conditions in the US during the decade of the 2000s, and the American Heart Association estimates that over a third of Americans currently suffer from some form of CVD. Worldwide, CVD is considered the fastest growing NCD health threat. For example, obesity has reached epidemic levels in some developing countries, as the populations have developed a growing penchant for western-style diets that pre-dispose to metabolic syndrome and its disease sequelae. In the CNS area, the WHO projects that by 2020, depression will be the second leading cause of disability worldwide.

Despite the enormous market opportunity in the CV and CNS space, the number of NAS approvals in these areas is static or declining; CV and CNS combined equal only about half the number of oncology approvals in 2013–2017. Whereas, the recent dominance of oncology approvals is largely a US phenomenon (82% of oncology launches among global NASs from 2013 to 2017 were in the US), the facts that 58% of NASs worldwide originate in the US (148/256), and 47% of the worldwide pipeline is focused on oncology/immunology[3], highlight a global concern going forward.

It is worth noting that the growth in NAS launches of ID products (both therapeutic and prophylactic) represents a positive trend and suggests an alignment of private/public resources and public health needs. This trend is the result of two factors. The first is that ex-US output of NAS appears to have a better balance of therapeutic areas than that of the US. The second factor is that the pipeline investment in ID drugs has benefitted from strong public health advocacy—a type of advocacy fundamentally different from the patient-focused advocacy spearheaded by cancer patient organizations, such as the American Cancer Society, and those of other disease areas.

One example of the striking effectiveness of public health advocacy in ID is the creation of the Generating Antibiotic Incentives Now (GAIN) Act in the US, which resulted from the efforts of a stakeholder group of 50 healthcare and labor organizations, who petitioned the US Congress to address public health needs in the area of antibiotic resistance[4]. The GAIN Act allows for the expedited review and approval of new ID drugs, as well as 5 years of market exclusivity. The Act's effectiveness was highlighted in a 2017 US Government report, crediting the legislation with achieving 101 ID designations and six approvals <5 years into the program. Going forward, however, success in bringing new ID drugs to market is not guaranteed; it is dependent on FDA resources and political will.

## The Up And Down Sides of Facilitated Regulatory Pathways

The regulatory environment can have a sizeable impact on the introduction of innovative new medicines, especially in areas with high unmet medical needs but low market incentives. Whereas, the ability to set high prices for new drugs, and extend market exclusivity, act as "pull" incentives, in that they increase the likelihood of sufficient return on investment and spur new research and development (R&D) activity, regulatory initiatives aimed at speeding development and review times serve as equally powerful "push" incentives, in that they lower the financial and logistical barriers to market entry, and reduce the technical risk of product development.

The US FDA employs a full panoply of what are referred to as Facilitated Regulatory Pathways (FRPs), including (a) priority review (submissions receive a 6-month review time, compared to a 10-month standard review), (b) accelerated approval (conditional approval based on surrogate, or indirect measures of benefit), (c) fast track designation (increased access to scientific interaction with the FDA and rolling reviews of portions of product applications as they become ready), and (d) breakthrough therapy designation (BTD: includes fast track designation incentives and "all hands on deck" collaborative, cross-disciplinary engagement by the FDA).

Since 2000, oncology drugs have received 45% of all FRPs awarded by the FDA, representing 32% of all priority reviews, 53% of all accelerated approvals, and 50% of all fast track designation. This has contributed to industry's growing focus on oncology R&D, which has no doubt benefited from the expansive scientific knowledge base that exists due to the US National Institutes of Health (NIH) and academic medical centers' response in the 1970s to President Nixon's declaration of the "War on Cancer." To highlight the point, during the decades of the 1980s and the 1990s, when cancer discovery efforts were still germinating, oncology drugs only represented 5 and 12% of overall US new drug approvals, respectively. By the first decade of the 2000s, however, that number reached parity with CV drugs at 19%. And in the period 2010–17, oncology drugs represented 29% of new approvals, compared to 14% for ID drugs, and 12% each for CV and CNS drugs[5]. In sum, in recent years, oncology drugs have been a major beneficiary of FRPs, which has stimulated investment in oncology R&D.

Is there a downside to FRPs? It is worth remembering that regulatory oversight is, in many ways, a zero-sum game. Political will and public advocacy are often lacking to address unmet medical needs in certain critical areas, and resources at regulatory agencies are finite. The US FDA itself has opined that such imbalances can result in boosted performance in one area to the detriment of another, effectively "squeezing out" certain therapeutic areas. There is a critical need for open debate to ensure alignment of public policy with public health needs.

## What Needs To Be Done

### Prioritization

Regional and national commissions should be created to review medical priorities, resource demands, and policy initiatives to achieve desired goals. Commissions should include experts from government, academia, industry, patient advocacy, insurers, and medical practice. The commissions should assess their region's immediate and long-term health needs and review the innovation landscape to determine whether current public and private R&D efforts are appropriately focused and funded.

Within regulatory authorities, FRP offices should be created to triage new drug applications. To help subsidize these activities, sponsors of candidate drugs could pay an application fee to the regulatory authority. If the FRP office determines that a drug candidate is eligible for one or more special regulatory programs, the sponsor would be exempt from paying any additional fees beyond standard user fees.

## Emerging Sponsors

The new drug research and development landscape is shifting dramatically, from the dominance of traditional big pharma to the emergence of venture capital–backed smaller companies and "emerging sponsors," defined by the US FDA as the sponsor listed on the approval letter who is not a holder of a previously approved application. Sponsors are classified as "emerging" even if they have partnership or parent relationships with sponsors of a currently approved product. In recent years, ~40% of new drug and biologic approvals in the US were from emerging sponsors. Emerging sponsors share many of the same characteristics as start-up companies, in that they may have little or no experience with commercial drug development, the regulatory process, or product launch. Pharmaprojects reports that of ~4,000 pharmaceutical companies with active pipelines, 56% have just one or two products in the pipeline, tacitly qualifying them as emerging sponsors. An FDA study documents that emerging sponsors are more likely to have multicycle reviews, and are less likely to garner approvals (50% approval rate as compared with 80% for medium/large companies).

The relative lack of R&D experience of emerging sponsors highlights the need for institutional programs and courses that offer training in the drug development process. Several highly regarded programs currently exist, such as Tufts CSDD's Postgraduate Course in Clinical Pharmacology, Drug Development and Regulation; the IFAPP Academy-King's College London Medical Affairs in Medicines Development online course; the University of California: San Francisco's American Course in Drug Development and Regulatory Science; and the University of Basel's European Center for Pharmaceutical Medicine. These programs offer a broad yet comprehensive overview of the drug development and regulatory process.

## New Technologies

Oncology R&D has benefitted greatly from dramatic advances in our understanding of the immunologic and genetic bases of cancer. A majority of recently approved cancer drugs are considered among the most innovative genomically-targeted precision medicines. In the US, much of the growth in scientific knowledge can be traced directly back to a high number of research grants awarded by the National Institutes of Health that focus on immunology and cancer.

Despite remarkable advances in the oncology field, it is worth asking: In light of the increasing availability of prognostic and diagnostic technology available for CNS disorders, and promising new approaches in regenerative medicine to treat CVD, is the continued dominance of oncology/immunology out of balance with health needs, both economically and medically? According to Pharmaprojects, nearly 50% of the global R&D pipeline is focused on anti-cancer therapies (4232/8934 products in 2017). Some observers have suggested that this over-emphasis on oncology in global R&D pipelines is a misallocation of resources and has generated a surplus of competition in some relatively narrow cancer indications. Moreover, the likelihood of success for oncology product development is relatively low. In a 2016 analysis, SCRIP Pharma Intelligence determined that immuno-oncology is one of the least successful therapeutic areas in terms of Phase III projects moving on to a regulatory filing, with only a 40% transition probability, compared to 58% for all ~1,500 products included in the analysis.

The US FDA, the EMA, and other national regulatory authorities have relied on regulatory science (i.e., developing new tools, standards, and approaches to assess safety, efficacy, quality, and performance) to understand and incorporate advances in new technologies. Nonetheless, challenges persist in agencies' attempts to integrate the risk-benefit profile of drugs, biologics, and devices during the product's entire time on the market. The goal is to close the evidence gap between the information regulators require to make decisions regarding product approval, and the type of information increasingly used by the medical community, payers, and others charged with making patient health care decisions.

### Global Competition vs. Harmonization

Asia (arguably excluding Japan) has been one of the greatest beneficiaries of globalization. The region as a whole accounts for 40% of world trade, according to the 2017 BCG report *How Asia Can Win in the new Global Era*. Recently however, some shifts in global economic currents have become detectable. Although manufacturing will remain an important contributor to growth in Asia, export-led economic models are now under pressure in most of the region. One reason for the decline is that trade, whose contribution to global GDP grew from around 25% in the 1960s to more than 60% in 2008, has since stalled. Another factor is that Asia's previously enormous manufacturing cost advantages have shrunk, as wage growth has outpaced productivity.

Nonetheless, with 60% of the world's population, the Asia-Pacific region is a significant focus for pharmaceutical sales by both domestic and foreign firms. The region also appears poised to become a nexus for pharmaceutical production, especially for vaccines and generics. However, Asian policymakers and companies cannot rely excessively on export manufacturing. To remain competitive in the global marketplace and to meet the needs of its own burgeoning population, Asia-Pacific must nurture innovation, such as regenerative medicine, in research areas that offer promising advances for unmet medical needs through international collaboration, strategic partnerships, and global harmonization.

### Patient-Focused Drug Development

According to the US FDA, patient-focused drug development (PFDD) describes efforts to ensure that the review process benefits from a systematic approach to obtaining patient perspectives on disease severity and medical need. For example, in the CNS area, the FDA has proposed a new approach for Alzheimer's disease R&D that allows treatment of pre-symptomatic patients to slow the accumulation of substances in the body believed to be biomarkers of clinical disease, or to treat patients with early disease before functional impairment is apparent through an accelerated approval pathway on the basis of assessment of cognitive outcome alone. There is precedent for this type of PFDD from AIDS activism in the 1990s, during which the FDA and industry handled the risks through patient involvement in a meaningful process of informed consent.

For CNS drug development, in general, many major diseases and disorders may benefit from a PFDD approach. At a recent FDA meeting, patients with amyotrophic lateral sclerosis (ALS) argued emphatically that regulatory revamping is necessary to get research moving in the field, as there is only a single drug on the market for the disease (the orphan drug riluzole extends life of ALS patients by about 3 months). The ALS patients' recommendations were, in essence, a wish list for all unmet needs in CNS: (1) incentivize companies, in particular small companies that seem to populate this research area, by clarifying the regulatory pathway through guidance; (2) do not be overprotective of patients in terms of risk; (3) allow for abbreviated pre–investigational new drug toxicology testing; (4) permit the use of historical controls; (5) allow expanded access; (6) utilize accelerated approval; and (7) provide for a limited population designation under the guidance of supervising neurologists, as might occur under BTD.

Another condition that could benefit from a PFDD approach is obesity. The need was discussed at a George Washington University Stakeholder Panel in which it was suggested that obesity should be viewed as three conditions: obese but otherwise well; obese with risk factors; and obese and sick. In an Infectious Diseases Society of America approach, indications should be targeted to specific patient populations through Special Medical Use (SMU) designation to control off-label (and off-target) use, instead of risk evaluation and mitigation strategies (REMS), which were not designed for that purpose. Secondary end points should be added on the benefits side of the scale, such as effects on joint pain, urinary incontinence, sleep apnea, and mobility.

## The Way Forward

National regulatory authorities worldwide are responsible for protecting and promoting public health, yet they must often expend energy and resources reacting to public health emergencies and political pressure. They must engage with an increasingly global pharmaceutical enterprise, deal with growing patient activism, and leverage new technologies and social media, all the while remaining cognizant of national cost-containment pressures. Unfortunately, whereas the challenges have grown, the resources available to deal with them have remained the same or decreased. This disparity threatens to relegate the health problems that afflict the majority of patients at any given moment to secondary concerns. Innovation follows investment, and investors respond to the regulatory and economic climate. By continuing to emphasize PFDD, and by demonstrating regulatory flexibility in disease areas with high unmet need (beyond cancer, AIDS and orphan diseases), regulatory authorities can indirectly incentivize R&D in these important therapeutic areas.

There is no simple answer to how to stimulate innovation in therapeutic areas where the need is great but commercial incentives may be lacking. The solution requires a multi-stakeholder approach to identify demand and build consensus for change. Going forward, sponsors, regulators, policy makers, payers, academics, key opinion leaders, and, perhaps most importantly, patients, must work together to chart a course to a healthier future.

## Notes

1. *Adapted from The Pharmaceutical Industry and Global Health: Facts and Figures 2012*, International Federation of Pharmaceutical Manufacturers & Associations.

2. Metabolic-Endocrine, which appears as the second most common NAS therapeutic area, represents a composite category of drugs for endocrine diseases

(e.g., type 2 diabetes), metabolic diseases, and congenital enzyme deficiencies (including many orphan drugs for rare conditions).

3. *Decline and Fall of the Pharma Pipeline.* (2017). No. 3847. Available online at: https://scrip.pharmaintelligence.informa.com/SC098394/The-Decline-And-Fall-Of-The-Pharma-Pipeline (Accessed December 4, 2018).

4. *50 Organizations' Letter to Congress on the Urgent Need for New Antibiotics.* (2012). Available online at: https://dpeaflcio.org/wp-content/uploads/Antibiotics-Sign-On-Letter-022212-House-Version.pdf. (Accessed November 19, 2018).

5. *Unpublished Tufts CSDD Data,* Tufts CSDD Marketed Database, (2018).

# Illegal Drugs Will Be a Catalyst for Dramatic Scientific Innovation

*David Nutt*

*David Nutt is an English neuropsychopharmocologist specializing in the research of drugs that affect the brain and their impact on addiction, anxiety, and sleep. He is the Edmund J. Safra Chair in Neuropsychopharmacology at Imperial College, London.*

The issue of drug use and harm is one of the most compelling challenges of the current era. The so-called "war on drugs," in which the UN has tried to stamp out recreational drug use through attacking drug suppliers and drug users, has been fought for over 40 years at great economic social and human costs and despite being widely discredited it is still ongoing.

One less discussed impact of making drugs "illegal" under the UN Conventions and national legislation is the hugely negative impact this has had on research and clinical innovation, where illegal drugs can no longer be studied or used to develop medical treatments.

For many years I have argued that this impact is the worst censorship of research in the history of science and medicine, and that a more enlightened approach to "illegal" drugs will revolutionise medical science.

## Banning Drugs in the UK Made Them More Popular

The premise that banning certain drugs for medicinal use will reduce their recreational use is clearly flawed, yet it still underpins current UN and almost all national regulations. This applies to the control of many drugs that have proven medical benefits, such as cannabis, psychedelics, and MDMA (the chemical name for the recreational drug called ecstasy).

"An Enlightened Approach to 'Illegal' Drugs Will Revolutionise Medicine and Science," by David Nutt, ScienceNordic, October 16, 2018. Reprinted by permission.

Cannabis was considered a medicine for millennia, when in the 1930s, following pressure from the USA, it was decided that it should be removed from medicine in a vain attempt to limit recreational use.

In the ensuing 80 years, the number of people using cannabis in the western world increased at least twenty-fold, proving the premise underpinning the ban to be utterly wrong.

In reality there was never significant diversion from medical use to recreational use of cannabis nor is there ever likely to be. Similar social trends have been seen in all western countries and yet only The Netherlands has had the courage to face the facts and keep cannabis as a medicine. Though Germany, Belgium, and Spain, have recently allowed it.

## Drug Ban Has Limited Research and Treatments

The banning of the psychedelics such as psilocybin and LSD plus MDMA was also largely a gesture to pressure from the US and the UN, fuelled by media hysteria over grossly exaggerated harms.

There is little, if any, evidence that the ban reduced recreational use and yet it has severely impeded these drugs from being used as medicines and research tools.

Before their ban, both psilocybin and MDMA were used successfully in therapy. But the case of LSD is perhaps the most outrageous.

## LSD: Most Effective Treatment for Alcoholism

Today, LSD is illegal in over 200 countries that have signed up to the UN Conventions.

Before it was banned in the late 1960s the US government had funded over 130 separate studies on LSD, with positive outcomes in many psychiatric disorders including anxiety, depression, and alcoholism in particular.

The founder of Alcoholics Autonomous (AA), Bill Wilson, achieved abstinence from alcoholism through a psychedelic experience. After this, he strongly supported the use of LSD to allow alcoholics to break free from the chains of their addiction.

Due to his enthusiasm, six trials of LSD to treat alcoholism were conducted. These have recently been subjected to modern statistical analysis by two Norwegian researchers who showed that the LSD treatment was more effective than any current treatments for alcoholism.

But since the 1967 ban, not a single person in the world has been allowed this treatment because all countries have signed up to the UN Conventions that state LSD has no medical value, and it was placed in Schedule 1 [the most severely controlled section] of the regulations, meaning that research was virtually impossible.

As well as being blatantly dishonest, these Conventions stopped all research in this area, for since the ban neither the US or UK governments have funded a single study on LSD.

Currently, more than three million people a year die prematurely from alcohol misuse according to WHO. Based on these figures I estimate conservatively that since 1967 over 100 million people world-wide have died prematurely from alcoholism, a disease that typically reduces life expectancy by 15-20 years. If LSD treatment had been continued we might expect at least 10 per cent of these to have become abstinent, saving around 10 million premature deaths.

Meanwhile, MDMA, which is illegal across all the world for recreational use, has recently been shown to have efficacy in the treatment of severe PTSD, where other conventional treatments have failed. Here again, just two MDMA sessions has been shown to produce powerful benefits lasting many years.

## Reverse the Ban on Schedule 1 Drugs

I would argue that the UN Conventions preventing such therapeutic benefits is the worst censorship of medicine in history, and totally disproportionate to the perceived benefits of the ban.

So how can we overturn this block on research and clinical treatments with these Schedule 1 drugs?

I believe that the way forward is to use a mixture of science and clinical trials. And in recent years a few scientists have tried to swing the pendulum back.

Our brain imaging studies of psilocybin (magic mushrooms juice) and LSD have shown the profound effect of these drugs to disrupt potentially maladaptive brain circuits and thinking processes that are now known to underlie disorders such as depression, addiction, and OCD.

These discoveries led us to apply for—and obtain—the first ever grant awarded by the UK Medical Research Council to study psilocybin. This allowed us to conduct a study of people with resistant depression and we found a very powerful and enduring antidepressant effect with just a single active dose.

Two similar studies in the USA have also found a similar efficacy in people with end of life depression and anxiety.

## Time We All Reconsidered

In light of these exciting and powerful findings I think it is time that all countries reviewed their own (seemingly) unthinking support of the current UN approach to recreational drug control, including the Nordics.

The war on drugs does much more harm than good and is hugely detrimental to medical research.

It is time for the people who might benefit from a repeal of these Schedules in all countries, to call on their politicians to review their national laws on these drugs and empower much more research in this area.

Let logic and evidence prevail!

# We Need to Study and Collect Data on Medical Marijuana

*David Trilling*

*David Trilling was a staff writer at* Journalist's Resource *from 2016 to 2018. He has written for* Foreign Affairs, Foreign Policy, *the* Nation, *the* Guardian, *and other publications.*

As marijuana use becomes ever more socially and legally acceptable in the developed world, researchers are scrambling to understand how the plant—more potent today than ever before—impacts our health. Marijuana is now legal in 28 U.S. states for medical use and in eight for recreation. But policy has far outpaced science, with almost every clinical study calling for further inquiry and many researchers complaining their work is stymied by federal regulations, which still treat cannabis as an illegal substance.

Judging by the available research, ample evidence exists to say that marijuana can treat pain, nausea and multiple sclerosis. It can harm lungs and the developing adolescent brain. Under certain circumstances, it can be addictive and increase the likelihood of auto accidents, low birth weight and, in cases of heavy use, schizophrenia.

The open questions about marijuana and its derivatives are far more numerous. How do benefits balance against side effects? How well can these substances treat seizures? How exactly do they affect the brain? How dangerous are the barely regulated chemicals used in processing weed for commercial use, like butane, pesticides and food additives? What other regulatory loopholes could lead to dangerous effects on consumers?

Without more rigorous study, these questions will remain unanswered and new ones will crop up, leaving policymakers and citizens to argue based on piecemeal research and personal convictions instead of adequate empirical data.

## What's In It and How It's Used

Cannabis has dozens of chemical compounds unique to the plant, known as cannabinoids. The one most famous for the high it gives is tetrahydrocannabinol (THC). But another one, cannabidiol (CBD), is largely non-psychoactive and is often the focus of research on marijuana's medicinal properties: It may lessen the frequency and intensity of seizures and may even improve cognitive function in adults. Medical marijuana is generally higher in CBD. Both THC and CBD are present in the cannabis plant as inactive acids. Heating—whether by smoking, vaporizing, baking, infusion or other methods—transforms them into active compounds.

## What We Know

A January 2017 report by the National Academies of Sciences, Engineering, and Medicine reviews most of the known research published since 1999 about marijuana and its impacts on health, making for one of the most comprehensive reads available. "The Health Effects of Cannabis and Cannabinoids" draws almost 100 conclusions, arguing that enough evidence exists to declare that marijuana can be used to treat pain, chemotherapy-induced nausea, and multiple sclerosis.

The report finds substantial evidence that marijuana use may: worsen respiratory function and cause bronchitis (when smoked); increase the likelihood of car accidents; and cause heavy users to develop schizophrenia. It also shows that males who both smoke cigarettes and use marijuana are more likely to develop an addiction to weed than either females or those who don't smoke cigarettes. Starting to use marijuana before age 16 also raises the risk of addiction. For expectant mothers, considerable evidence suggests that marijuana can negatively impact birthweight.

The report finds moderate evidence: that marijuana use impairs learning, memory and attention, especially in adolescents;

that it may improve cognitive performance among some people with certain psychotic disorders; and that it does not worsen schizophrenia. (There is no evidence it can treat the disorder.)

No known association has been found with lung cancer and there is limited evidence that marijuana use increases the risk of heart attacks.

## Why We Don't Know More

One problem in compiling the report, and in exploring the health effects of marijuana more generally, is a dearth of studies and funding for research because of federal regulations, said the lead author, Marie McCormick, during a March 2017 event at Harvard's T.H. Chan School of Public Health.

For one thing, researchers complain about their limited legal access to real weed, the kind people outside of labs use: "It is often difficult for researchers to gain access to the quantity, quality, and type of cannabis product necessary to address specific research questions on the health effects of cannabis use," the National Academies report declares.

The Drug Enforcement Agency (DEA) classifies marijuana as a Schedule I narcotic. By definition, that means, like heroin, it is highly prone to abuse and has no medical purpose—a rating that *Scientific American* has called "highly controversial and dubious." So researchers cannot simply use what they might buy on a street corner or even at a pot shop in states where it is legal under local laws.

The plant clinical researchers do use comes from a farm at the University of Mississippi that the National Institute on Drug Abuse (NIDA) licenses to grow marijuana for research purposes. But scientists complain that what they receive is far less potent than marijuana consumed by the public and even looks like an entirely different plant. The result, *The Washington Post* declared in 2017, is "akin to investigating the effects of bourbon by giving people Bud Light."

In August 2016, the DEA announced it would loosen control over the cultivation of government marijuana, though it remains unclear when the changes will go into effect.

Other difficulties studying the effects of marijuana relate to metrics. There is no standard definition of what constitutes frequent use, moderate use or low use, noted Staci Gruber of McLean Hospital at the Harvard event. Researchers have yet to look closely at the effects of marijuana use on those who smoke or eat it once or twice a month. Federal health surveys, moreover, do not ask detailed questions of users.

## Kids and Pot

One question that has loomed large as more places have legalized marijuana use is, "How bad is it for children?"

Two recent studies observe that regular marijuana use is likely much worse for children before age 16 than it is for adults. A 2015 study in *Developmental Cognitive Neuroscience* found that kids who start using marijuana before age 16 may have lower cognitive function than people who start using later: "Given that the brain undergoes significant development during adolescence and emerging adulthood and that the frontal cortex is among the last of the brain regions to mature, it is perhaps not surprising that individuals with earlier exposure to [marijuana] have difficulty with tasks requiring frontal/executive function." A 2014 study in *Psychopharmacology* also found a correlation between smoking marijuana and impulsive behavior, especially among those who begin regular use before they turn 16.

Marijuana bred for high levels of THC often has less CBD. A 2017 study found CBD may act as a safety mechanism, especially among adolescents.

Other research includes studies on addiction, IQ and the links between legalization and usage:

- One 2017 review in *The Lancet* notes that while about 1 in 11 people who use marijuana will develop a dependence, that number almost doubles among people who started as adolescents.

- A 2011 study of twins—where one uses pot and one does not—finds no evidence to associate the drug with a lower IQ, though it calls for more research.
- A 2016 study in *Drug and Alcohol Dependence* analyzes the design of medical marijuana laws and use by adolescents. Looking at 45 states, it finds slightly higher use of marijuana among teenagers in states where medical marijuana is legal (22.7 percent in the previous 30 days) compared to states where it is not (19.8 percent). But after adjusting for demographics and other factors, the authors discover a small decline in adolescent use in those states where medical marijuana is legal.
- Research in Washington and Colorado before and after recreational marijuana was legalized in both states in 2012 found perceptions of its harmfulness fell among youth in Washington but not in Colorado, where medical marijuana had already been well-established. Eighth- and 10th-grade students in Washington increased their usage over the same period; youth marijuana consumption in Colorado did not appear to change, the authors report in *JAMA Pediatrics*.

The Canadian Pediatric Society in 2016 released a position statement recommending that Ottawa—where full recreational legalization is being considered—take a number of steps to keep marijuana out of the hands of anyone younger than 18 and regulate the amount of THC in legal marijuana products.

## "Dang, That's Strong!"

It's not your parents' grass anymore: The marijuana available today is many times more potent than it was in the days of "Reefer Madness" or Woodstock. In 2015, the American Chemical Society reported that THC content in some marijuana strains had roughly tripled in three decades.

One of the most potent products on the market is butane hash oil, sometimes known as marijuana wax. Used in increasingly popular "vape pens" and in the production of edibles, it is made by passing butane (a liver-damaging, explosive and all-around dangerous hydrocarbon gas) through marijuana buds to make a viscous liquid and then evaporating off some of the butane. It is illegal in many states. Not only is the production process dangerous, but smoking "wax made with butane leaves small molecules that adhere to the lungs and creates a black spot much like miners' lung," says a handout from the Department of Health and Human Services.

## Medical Marijuana

With medical marijuana now available in more than half of US states and a growing number of countries, the plant is being used to treat all sorts of ailments including pain and chemotherapy side-effects such as nausea, loss of appetite, and insomnia (even as doctors complain they lack dosing guidelines). Each of these uses is addressed (and generally endorsed) in the 2017 National Academies report.

A major area of study is the use of medical marijuana in treating epileptic seizures, discussed separately below. Other research has explored its effects on cognitive function, on the use of opiates and on the use of recreational marijuana:

- One 2016 study in *Frontiers in Pharmacology* finds signs that medical marijuana may help improve cognitive function in adults. The researchers suspect this is because some medical marijuana products contain higher amounts of CBD and other cannabinoids than does recreational marijuana, "which may mitigate the adverse effects of THC on cognitive performance."
- Some scholars see a decline in the use and abuse of opiates by cannabis users, though the National Academies report uncovers no evidence to support or refute this finding.

- Writing in *JAMA Internal Medicine* in 2014, Marcus Bachhuber of the Philadelphia Veterans Affairs Medical Center and his colleagues find "medical cannabis laws are associated with significantly lower state-level opioid overdose mortality rates." Patients seem to be using marijuana as an opioid substitute; marijuana is far less addictive and dangerous than drugs derived from the opium poppy. A 2016 study by Columbia University researchers confirms those findings and observes that states with medical-marijuana laws have fewer opioid-related car accidents.

- A 2015 study sees an association between medical marijuana and the lower use of addictive opioids as pain medication; it also reports fewer opioid-related deaths. At the same time, the paper finds a correlation between the availability of medical marijuana and higher rates of recreational marijuana use.

A 2017 study in *Drug and Alcohol Dependence* finds no indication that CBD, the "medical" cannabinoid, might be addictive.

## Treating Epilepsy

The fast-growing body of research suggests that CBD—now sometimes called Charlotte's Web after a CBD-based medicine that reportedly helped a severely ill child—might alleviate treatment-resistant seizures among epilepsy patients. In 2013 the Food and Drug Administration (FDA) allowed tests of Epidiolex, a CBD oil concentrate developed by GW Pharmaceuticals, which is not yet commercially available.

In 2016, the American Epilepsy Society (AES) called on the federal government to support further research into the use of marijuana to treat the neurological disorder. "Robust scientific evidence for the use of marijuana is limited. The lack of information does not mean that marijuana is ineffective for epilepsy. It merely means that we do not know if marijuana is a safe and effective treatment for epilepsy, which is why it should be studied using the well-founded research methods that all other effective treatments for epilepsy have undergone," the AES statement says.

It also calls on the DEA to review its classification of marijuana as a Schedule I drug: "AES's call for rescheduling is not an endorsement of the legalization of marijuana, but is a recognition that the current restrictions on the use of medical marijuana for research continue to stand in the way of scientifically rigorous research into the development of cannabinoid-based treatments."

A 2016 study of CBD in *Lancet Neurology* finds a 36.5 percent decline in monthly seizures among 162 patients suffering severe, childhood-onset, treatment-resistant epilepsy. The trial was open, meaning patients knew what they were receiving, which is not a preferred way to do medical research; the authors call for randomized controlled trials. Besides the decline in seizures, they find side effects including fatigue, diarrhea, decreased appetite and convulsions.

A number of recent studies—such as a 2017 paper in *Epilepsy Behavior* and a 2014 paper in *Epilepsia*—summarize the research and anecdotal evidence that CBD can help control epileptic seizures. They both call for randomized, controlled research trials that are double-blind—i.e., where neither the patients nor the doctors know who is receiving the drug and who is receiving a placebo.

The National Academies report takes a dimmer view of the available clinical data, noting that it consists "solely of uncontrolled case series, which do not provide high-quality evidence of efficacy." It acknowledges the need for more research into CBD's potential effect on neurological disorders such as epilepsy and seizures, but concludes that "there is insufficient evidence to support or refute the conclusion that cannabinoids are an effective treatment for epilepsy."

## Regulations, Pesticides, Food Production

Some of the biggest holes in research concern the production of marijuana and its derivatives, including the use of pesticides and the preparation of edibles. Like other deficits in research they stem in part from the disconnect between federal and state laws on marijuana.

In agriculture, pesticides are usually regulated by federal bodies such as the Environmental Protection Agency and approved for specific crops after the pesticide manufacturer pays for testing that the EPA deems reliable. But because the EPA is a federal agency, it will not label a chemical safe for marijuana. So regulation is handled by individual states, which often lack the capacity to investigate problematic pesticides. State governments "have never been made to play the detective role in this," Andrew Freedman, the former director of the Office of Marijuana Coordination for the state of Colorado, tells Journalist's Resource.

States where marijuana is legal have been known to recall batches believed to have been exposed to unapproved pesticides such as the insecticides imidacloprid or pyrethrin. (Some states have websites with regulatory information, including California, Colorado and Washington.) Some researchers, meanwhile, express concern about lobbying by the chemical industry to weaken pesticide regulations. Very little has been published about the effects of marijuana pesticides on human health.

Another area in need of study is the production of edibles. The FDA has not approved any product containing CBD as a dietary supplement, but, at the time of writing, has not aggressively enforced federal laws that the FDA interprets to ban marijuana compounds in food.

Marijuana marketing is another topic worthy of greater scrutiny. A 2015 commentary in *The New England Journal of Medicine* sounds the alarm about the popularity of edible snacks containing THC that are "packaged to closely mimic popular candies and other sweets." Citing the risk of consumption by children, the authors, two researchers at Stanford, call on the federal government and the courts to regulate the sale of edibles.

## Other Resources

The number of American cannabis users is rising. According to an August 2016 Gallup Poll, 13 percent of Americans say they use the drug, up from 7 percent in 2007. Slightly older data from the National Survey on Drug Use and Health, published by the US Department of Health and Human Services, say over 22 million Americans aged 12 or older have used marijuana in the past month. That is 8.4 percent of the population.

CannabisWire.com, The Cannabist, and *High Times* magazine are among the news outlets that cover the growing legal marijuana business. Pot beats and pot critics are increasingly common at traditional newspapers.

For *Scientific American* in 2016, David Downs wrote a history of the federal government's "war" on marijuana. Downs, the cannabis editor at the *San Francisco Chronicle*, has also penned a glossary of marijuana terminology.

Journalist's Resource has reviewed literature on how crime and drunk driving tend to fall after marijuana legalization. We also have looked at potential tax revenue from legal weed.

The National Institute on Drug Abuse regularly updates its fact sheet on marijuana.

# Removing Long-Time Barriers to Research and Medical Innovation

*David Nutt*

*David Nutt is an English neuropsychopharmocologist specializing in the research of drugs that affect the brain and their impact on addiction, anxiety, and sleep. He is the Edmund J. Safra Chair in Neuropsychopharmacology at Imperial College, London.*

Many drugs are made "illegal" in an attempt to reduce their availability and so their harms. This control occurs at both national and international levels—in the latter case, in the United Nations conventions that make a whole range of drugs from cannabis to heroin "illegal." Many people are aware of the challenges to this system of control in terms of human rights abuses by those who seek to implement a prohibitionist approach to drug control, as well as the failure of, and massive collateral damage from, the "War on Drugs" that is currently being waged to stop drug use. Less well known are the perverse restrictions that these laws have had on pharmacology and therapeutics research. Here I will show how they have led to censoring of life science and medical research, with disastrous consequences that have lasted for more than 50 years and counting.

Recently additional controls have started to be developed, provoked by the fear of so-called "legal highs." These are drugs that mimic the actions of controlled drugs but are of different chemical structures, so they fall outside the UN conventions or local laws. So, for example, the Republic of Ireland has now banned the sale of any chemical that might be used recreationally, a move that if enforced could stop all pharmaceutical research and development in the country. In the United States, city and state governments often move to outlaw novel drugs before the federal government believes

Nutt D (2015), "Illegal Drugs Laws: Clearing a 50-Year-Old Obstacle to Research." PLOS Biology 13(1): e1002047. https://doi.org/10.1371/journal.pbio.1002047

it has sufficient evidence to make that determination. Some have been extreme in their lack of understanding of pharmacology. For example, a bill in Maryland would have outlawed any compound with any binding to any cannabinoid receptor, with no mention of thresholds for binding affinity, whether the ligand had agonist or antagonist efficacy, or whether actions at other receptor sites might moderate overall abuse potential. This demonstrates a very extreme version of prohibition, in which molecular entities that have yet to exist are deemed Schedule 1, as if we had absolute ability to perfectly predict the activity of a novel chemical structure.

## Drug Control Laws

Most national laws controlling "illegal" drugs are based on the UN Single Convention on Narcotic Drugs (1961) and the Convention on Psychotropic Substances (1971) that define a range of substances that are supposedly sufficiently harmful to be removed from the usual sales regulations. They are made "illegal," which means that punishments are implemented for sale and, in most cases, possession. Some of these can be very severe; e.g., some countries have the death penalty for personal possession of heroin and other opioids [1].

However, many "illegal" drugs have medicinal uses: for example, opioids for pain, amphetamines for narcolepsy and attention deficit hyperactivity disorder (ADHD), and even cocaine for local blood control and anaesthesia in ear nose and throat (ENT) surgery. In most Western countries there is an attempt to make the medical use of these exempt from the legal controls that try to limit recreational use. So, in the United Kingdom and US, drugs such as morphine and amphetamine are exempted from the most severe controls that apply to non-medical drugs, such as crack cocaine and crystal meth (see [1]). In practice this means that they are available from pharmacies and most universities can hold them for research purposes.

The problem for researchers comes from two sources: (1) the banning of certain medicines and (2) current regulations limiting the study of the medical potential of drugs, e.g. LSD, psilocybin, and MDMA, that are subject to the most stringent level of control.

## The Banning of Certain Medicines

Many traditional medicines have been defined out of the pharmacopeia by international and national conventions. These include plant sources of DMT such as ayahausca and ibogaine, but the most obvious one is cannabis. Cannabis has been used medically for over 4,000 years [2], yet since the 1961 UN Single Convention on Narcotic Drugs, it has been defined as not having such value. As a result, cannabis is put into Schedule 1. Drugs located in Schedule 1 are subject to the most stringent level of control in most countries in the world (see [1] for a fuller description of these schedules and laws justifying them). This status means that researchers (both preclinical and clinical) require a special licence to hold the drug. In the UK only four (out of many hundred) hospitals have such a licence, though all can hold heroin, a much more harmful and sought-after drug by anyone's estimate, because heroin is in Schedule 2. These restrictions have meant that research on the medical uses of cannabis has hardly occurred in the past 50 years, despite substantial increase in knowledge of the many pharmacologically active components of the cannabis plant, many of which have medical potential [2]. Moreover, what little research has taken place—such as the development of the cannabis oral spray Sativex—has been delayed by the question of what licence it would be given (now in the UK, it is Schedule 4 despite being identical in pharmaceutical content to plant cannabis, which is still held in Schedule 1].

Similar controls apply in the US, where therapeutic studies on cannabis products have been hampered by intense regulations: in the US only three people hold Drug Enforcement Agency licences to research cannabis clinically. As a result, in many US states the population defied Federal laws and voted for the legalization of medical cannabis (with Colorado and Washington State making recreational use legal as well).

In the UK sub-national democracy for health issues does not exist, so it is estimated that over 30,000 people use medical cannabis illegally, and many get arrested for doing so, particularly as, since 2005, self-medication with cannabis has been specifically excluded as a defence in UK law (despite the fact that it can still be pleaded as a defence for the use of any other "illegal" drug for self-medication) [3].

## How the Law Stops Innovation of New Medicines

Many popular "illegal" drugs have plausible medical uses. Some of these come from studies that were conducted when they were legal. For instance, LSD was tested in six clinical trials for alcoholism before it was banned in the 1960s. A recent meta-analysis of these studies found an effect-size equal to that of any current treatment for this addiction [4]. So why has the therapeutic potential of LSD not been developed for the past 50 years? The answer is that, because of its Schedule 1 status, research is almost impossible. Most hospitals are banned from holding it, as are many university research institutions. Getting a Schedule 1 licence in the UK takes about a year and costs around £5,000, with £3,000 for the licence and £2,000 for the other requirements such as extra security for the drug cabinets, police checks, etc.

Additionally, there is often considerable extra bureaucracy with the need and cost of import licences, since most suppliers are overseas. Moreover, sourcing an LSD formulation for human clinical trial use is close to impossible under current UK and European clinical trial guidelines that require Good Manufacturing Practice (GMP) production compliance, as no company we know of in the world is currently approved for this. The situation is somewhat easier in the US and Switzerland, where drugs sourced to high purity, though without the full GMP accreditation, can be used in clinical studies (see [1]). Thus, academic chemistry departments and small chemistry producers can act as providers.

Similar considerations apply to other drugs, although the rising interest in psilocybin as a neuroscience tool and as a possible treatment for obsessive compulsive disorder (OCD) [5] and depression has led to one company developing a GMP supply. However, this does not end the regulatory hurdles as the tableting and dispensing still requires a Schedule licenced site, which are scarce, and as mentioned above, only four hospitals in the UK have a Schedule 1 dispensing licence. Our own experience has shown that overcoming these hurdles—if at all possible—takes several years and increases the cost of this research by about 10-fold over that for "legal" drugs.

The regulations can also be applied arbitrarily to new drugs that are under research. For example, based on the clinical case reports of MDMA helping in the dyskinesia of Parkinson's disease [6] we began to develop a series of legal MDMA analogues for this indication. In parallel, "head-shops" began selling similar analogues for recreational use. Following some media hysteria, these drugs became banned in the UK, but the legislation was vey broad and so included the compounds we were working on [7]. As a result, this research has now had to stop because not all the various sites on which the work was conducted can afford Schedule 1 licences.

Another recent example is that of ketamine analogues that were being developed as new treatments for pain and depression [1, 8]. Because one or two became available for recreational use (though without any deaths), these and hundreds of other analogues were banned and put in Schedule 1. This effectively stopped research in this field, leaving only ketamine (as it is Schedule 2) available for research. Ketamine is well known to be dependence inducing and to produce significant bladder damage in a proportion of users, so finding safer alternatives was a priority; the fact that all known analogues, including many that may never be developed—let alone tested—are now Schedule 1 drugs means that finding a safer alternative is now almost certainly never going to happen. The pharmaceutical industry is very reluctant to develop drugs that are controlled because of the significant cost implications of the regulatory hurdles and because investors often consider working in the "illegal" drug space to be condoning drug abuse.

One further absurdity of the current approach is that it takes no notice of amount. This means that a single molecule of an "illegal" drug is illegal. This is already limiting PET research with new 5HT2A receptor tracers, where picogramme quantities required for tracer production (well below quantities having psychological effects) need licences [7]. Similarly, research on the epidemiology of new psychoactive substances is limited because once they are made illegal, transferring tiny (sub-active) amounts between research labs becomes subject to complex licence and import–export regulations. In the UK such licences are required for each and every drug separately which massively increases costs. Moreover each are time-limited to only 8 weeks so they need to be renewed repeatedly.

Our work on cannabis has been delayed because it turned out that cannabis placebo is considered a Schedule 1 drug in the UK. This meant that placebo had to be added to our licence and that import and export licences were then required for obtaining it from overseas suppliers. As these licences only last for 8 weeks, they commonly time-expire before the university or the supplier have dealt with the contractual documents. We are currently on our third licence for placebo cannabis and still awaiting supply.

Most researchers do not have the time, money, or energy to work their way through the regulatory jungle. We are the first group in the UK ever to study psilocybin and the first in the 50 years since the regulations were brought in to study LSD. Already the insights gained have transformed our understanding of the role of these drugs and, by inference, the role of 5HT2A receptors in brain function [9], and these findings have now been back-translated into preclinical studies with considerable value [10].

Maybe one could argue that the impairment of research produced by the regulations on "illegal" drugs is worth it because recreational use is reduced. However, it is highly doubtful that this is the case with any of these drugs since they are all readily available from dealers or even over the Internet. Moreover, we can find no instances of diversion of Schedule 1 or Schedule 2 drugs from research labs. So the law simply censors research rather than protects the public; indeed the limitation to clinical research produced by the regulations almost certainly has done much more harm than good to society by impeding medical progress.

## What Is the Solution?

This is remarkably simple; all that needs to happen is for each national government to redefine UN Schedule 1 drugs as Schedule 2 in their country. The governments would still be complying with the UN conventions (i.e., the drugs would still be "illegal"), but the drugs could be held by research establishments and hospitals alongside drugs currently in Schedule 2, e.g., opioids and stimulants. There would be no increased risk of diversion, but a significant easing of the regulatory burden for research. A more rational European approach to GMP production of research compounds for Phase I and II clinical trials would also make clinical research much easier without any significant risk to participants.

As we work towards lifting the ban on pharmacological innovation and research with current Schedule 1 drugs, it will be important to encourage and support the efforts of scientists to oppose harmful new legislation, such as blanket bans on chemical or pharmacological series. In the US, researchers have intervened in these political processes when city-based or state-based proposed legislation has threatened current or upcoming medical research projects.

## References

1.  Nutt DJ, King LA, Nichols DE (2013) Effects of Schedule I drug laws on neuroscience research and treatment innovation. Nat Rev Neurosci. 14(8):577–85. Epub 2013 Jun 12. . pmid:23756634

2.  Pertwee R (2014) Handbook of Cannabis. Oxford: Oxford University Press.

3.  Nutt DJ (2010) Necessity or nastiness? The hidden law denying cannabis for medical use. http://profdavidnutt.wordpress.com/2010/12/13/necessity-or-nastiness-the-hidden-law-denying-cannabis-for-medicinal-use/. 13 December 2010.

4.  Krebs T, Johansen P-Ø (2012) Lysergic acid diethylamide (LSD) for alcoholism: a meta-analysis of controlled trials. J. Psychopharmacol. 26: 994–1002. pmid:22406913

5.  Moreno FA, Wiegand CB, Taitano EK, Delgado PL (2006) Safety, tolerability and efficacy of psilocybin in 9 patients with obsessive-compulsive disorder. J. Clin. Psychiatry 67, 1735–1740. pmid:17196053

6.  Huot PH, Johnston TH, Lewis KD, Koprich JB, Reyes G, Fox SH, Piggott MJ, Brotchie JM (2011) Characterization of 3,4-methylenedioxymethamphetamine (MDMA) enantiomers *in vitro* and in the MPTP-lesioned primate: *R*-MDMA reduces severity of dyskinesia, whereas *S*-MDMA extends duration of ON-time. J. Neurosci. 31, 7190–7198. pmid:21562283

7.  Nutt DJ, King LA, Nichols DE (2013). New victims of current drug laws. Nat Rev Neurosci 14: 877. pmid:24149187

8.  Coppola M, Mondola R (2012) Methoxetamine: from drug of abuse to rapid-acting antidepressant. Med. Hypotheses 79, 504–507. pmid:22819129

9.  Carhart-Harris RL, Erritzoe D, Williams T, Stone JM, Reed LJ, et al. (2012) Neural correlates of the psychedelic state as determined by fMRI studies with psilocybin. Proc. Natl Acad. Sci. USA 109, 2138–2143. pmid:22308440

10. Riga MS, Soria G, Tudela R, Artigas F, Celada P (2014) The natural hallucinogen 5-MeO-DMT, component of ayahuasca, disrupts cortical function in rats. International Journal of Neuropsychopharmacology, 17, 1269–1282. pmid:24650558

# Science Defines Medical Cannabis Today

*Dr. C. M. Helm-Clark*

*Dr. Helm-Clark is a retired scientist and consultant with experience in fieldwork and geothermal mapping. She is a freelance writer focused on health and life sciences, toxicology, and material sciences. She operates the blog* Gnarly Science.

What is medical marijuana? That might be a moot question in a place like California, but I don't live in a blue state. I live in a red state without laws that legalize medical marijuana. Because some of my regular audience lives where I do, we'll first define some terms and explain some concepts. I find that a lot of conservative-state folks are not familiar with what the medical marijuana thing is really about.

Today we look at what medical marijuana is and isn't. We will also look at how the federal government has regulated research on cannabis.

## Medical Marijuana Defined

According to the US government, the term *medical marijuana* refers to using marijuana or its extracts to treat symptoms or causes of illness.

- Defining the term does not imply approval. At this time, the federal government doesn't approve of this practice.
- The US Food and Drug Administration (FDA) does not recognize or approve marijuana as medicine. The cannabis plant and its direct derivatives remain a Schedule I agent. That means it is legally classified as: "a drug with a high potential for abuse, and no currently accepted medical use."

## Cannabinoids

"Medical marijuana" includes more than just the cannabis plant itself. It also includes substances derived from the plant. These derivatives are often labeled as cannabinoids. This usage is actually a slight misuse of the term. Initially, in the medical literature, *cannabinoid* referred to the distinct biochemicals isolated from cannabis. When you read that there are more than a hundred biologically-active cannabinoids, this is an example of the original use of the term.

In the politicized language of drug policy, the term cannabinoid has expanded over the last two decades. Its current usage also includes substances like cannabis-resin extracts. In addition, compounds of more than one cannabis biochemical such as THC+CBD capsules are also called cannabinoids. This latter usage treats the term as a catch-all for anything extracted from the plant.

## Cannabinoids Used in Medical Studies

The following is a brief list of some of the important medical-marijuana cannabinoids.

- THC: The main ingredient in marijuana is *delta-9-tetrahydrocannabinol*, better known as THC. This is the stuff that makes people "high."
- CBD: This is an acronym for the cannabis-derived biochemical *cannabidiol*. Unlike THC, it has no intoxicating effects.
  - It is used in Epidiolex, a prescription drug legal in the UK for the treatment of certain seizure disorders. Currently, Epidiolex is in clinical trials in the United States for the treatment of two severe forms of childhood epilepsy, Dravet syndrome and Lennox-Gastaut syndrome.
  - CBD is sold in various forms as an unregulated supplement. This practice occurs in some states like Colorado which have liberal medical-use laws or have legalized recreational use.

- THC Capsules, CBD Capsules, and THC/CBD Capsules: These are capsules sold by some medical marijuana dispensaries. They are made by concentrating THC and/or CBD into an oil. The oil is then put into a standard gelatin capsule and sold. The dose and content of different capsule brands are variable.

## Cannabinoids Not Included in Clinical Studies

These are important. The cannabinoids which are *not* studied form a large portion of what is sold as medical marijuana. Because they are not studied, claims of their medical benefits stand on questionable ground.

- Cannabis Concentrates: There are numerous ways to concentrate THC, CBD and other cannabinoids out of a cannabis plant. The different methods result in different products. All of them, though, share one property: they take the bioactive chemicals out of the plant and concentrate them in an edible, inhalable, or absorbable form.

  · Hash is a concentrate made by collecting and compressing of the resin and/or powdery kief (resin glands) from the cannabis plant.

  · BHO stands for butane hash oil. Cannabinoids are stripped from the plant through butane extraction. The product left behind is a waxy substance that will harden into cannabis "wax," the glasslike "shatter" or the crumbly "honeycomb." When these BHO concentrates are heated on a nail head or other hot metal and then inhaled, they are sometimes called "daps."

  · $CO_2$ Oil is made by subjecting a cannabis plant to a pressured extraction process using carbon dioxide. The extract is an oil. The oil is commonly mixed with polypropylene glycol and loaded into a vape pen. The pen vaporizes the $CO_2$ oil-polypropylene glycol mixture which is then inhaled.

· RSO is Rick Simpson oil. Back in 2003, the Canadian Simpson made an oily cannabis extract by soaking cannabis in either light aliphatic naphtha or 99% isopropyl alcohol. He then concentrated the resulting amber-colored extract. He used the extract as a topical on his skin cancer which surgery had failed to eradicate. Simpson claims the topical application cured his cancer. People have since used RSO topically or orally in hopes of treating cancer and other ailments.

· Cannabis Tincture is made by extracting cannabinoids from cannabis plants with alcohol. Before they were banned in 1937, tinctures were the most popular form of cannabis-derived drugs.

## FDA-Approved Cannabinoid Drugs

- Dronabinol: This is a Schedule II FDA-approved drug used to treat nausea caused by chemotherapy.
  - · Dronabinol is synthetic THC. In prescription form, it is marketed as the branded drugs Marinol™ and Sybdros™.
- Nabilone: This is a Schedule III FDA-approved drug, also used to treat the GI-distress symptoms of chemotherapy.
  - · Nabilone is a synthetic cannabinoid with a structure similar to THC. It is sold as the branded medicine Cesamet™.
- Nabiximols is sold in Canada, the UK and several European countries as the branded drug Sativex®.
  - · Nabiximols is a 1:1 mix of THC and CBD.
  - · It treats muscle control problems caused by multiple sclerosis.

· It is not approved by the FDA for use in the United States.

## Commercially-Available Medical Marijuana Products

Medical marijuana businesses offer a wide variety of products:

- cannabis for smoking
- edible cannabis in chocolate or baked goods
- cannabis concentrates in vape pens
- cannabis concentrates for inhalation through dabbing
- THC, CBD and THC/CBD capsules
- cannabis tinctures

Medical marijuana businesses do not sell FDA-approved cannabinoid drugs. These drugs, listed above, have gone through the rigorous clinical trials required in the United States. You may not be aware of this but the bar for drug approval is higher in the USA than in a lot of other countries. Drug approval here takes longer than in many other places. Nothing sold in a medical marijuana dispensary has federal approval either as a prescription or as an over-the-counter drug.

## The Gap Between Medical Marijuana and NIDA-Approved Clinical Trials

The National Institute on Drug Abuse (NIDA) has a stranglehold on what clinical trials can use for research on cannabis and cannabinoids. Until 2016, clinical trials in the USA could only use:

- synthetic cannabinoids
- prescription drugs approved for treatments in other countries
- a limited amount of low-potency cannabis grown at the NIDA-approved facility at the University of Mississippi

While the amount of cannabis available for research was recently increased, the impediments are still profound. The quality of cannabis available for medical study is currently inferior to the cannabis available from any medical marijuana business. The THC-potency of modern illicit marijuana is higher than in the past. The cannabis available for research is grown from a less-potent strain from decades ago.

Research studies are constrained to use cannabis and plant-derived cannabinoids that are not at all equivalent to what is sold in medical marijuana businesses. This undermines the validity of correlations between research results and the potential effects of medical marijuana products.

## Regulatory Barriers to Research

In addition to the restriction in materials, any clinical study that wants to use cannabis or cannabinoids has additional barriers to overcome. Because marijuana and its derivatives are Schedule I drugs, there are also four additional regulatory agencies' worth of hoops to jump through. These requirements are in addition to the already-stiff FDA requirements. Not only is much more paperwork required for approval, cannabis-related research takes *years* longer than for any other class of drugs.

Regulatory barriers to medical studies are a large part of the disconnect between scientific research results on cannabis and the potential effects of medical marijuana.

Interested readers may want to consult the 2017 report by the National Academy of Science on medical marijuana. It has an excellent and detailed description of the problems introduced for cannabis research by the government's policies.

# Historically, Medical Experiments Led to Accidental Addiction

*Stevyn Colgan*

*Stevyn Colgan is an author, artist, and popular public speaker. He's one of the writers of the BBC TV series* QI *and BBC Radio's* The Museum of Curiosity. *Previously, he spent thirty years as a police officer in London.*

The lengths to which some drug addicts will go to assuage their needs are quite extreme. Many turn to crime to fund their supply, others to prostitution or even to forms of slavery. Once, when I was working as a police officer, I met a man who had self-tattooed the location of his blood vessels onto his arms. He'd done so because the places he would regularly visit to inject himself—public toilets, mostly—had been fitted with blue lighting that was designed to make it difficult for drug users to find their veins.

Intravenous (IV) intoxicants are the hardest of hard drugs. They provide an almost immediate "rush" as the drug enters the bloodstream and is carried to the brain. They also carry some of the highest risks.

> "An extraordinary spectacle was revealed on examination. The entire surface of the abdomen and lower extremities was covered with discoloured blotches, [...] the marks of the injections. He was spotted as a leopard. For four years he had averaged three or four a day—an aggregate of between five and six thousand blissful punctures!"
>
> Description of an intravenous drug user from Gibbons H. Letheomania: The result of the hypodermic injection of morphia. Pacific Medical and Surgical Journal 1870;12:481–95.

Nearly all of the drugs involved are addictive and they all result in fatality if the dose is too high. Supplies may be adulterated or "cut" with inferior fillers. Skin lesions and open wounds can lead to infection and disease. The accidental injection of air into a blood vessel (embolism) can be fatal. And using unclean or shared needles or other paraphernalia can spread viruses such as hepatitis C or HIV.

## Experiments and Breakthrough Discoveries

Intravenous drug abuse via syringe is a fairly modern phenomenon; the first recorded cases appeared in 1925, although some reports suggest that needle sharing was occurring in China as early as 1902, and could have been responsible for outbreaks of malaria in Egypt, the United States and China between 1929 and 1937. But that's because the hypodermic syringe as we know it today only appeared in the late 19th century.

However, the delivery of drugs directly into the bloodstream may have a history that goes back thousands of years, as our ancestors placed extracts from healing plants onto open wounds and lesions, or poured them into specially made incisions.

We know that Sir Christopher Wren, best known as the architect of St Paul's Cathedral in London, injected dogs with alcohol, opium and other substances to see what effect they had on the animals while he was at Wadham College, Oxford in 1656. His apparatus was a quill attached to a bladder containing the drug. To gain access to a vein, he had to make a cut in the skin.

He also attempted to inject a human subject, the "delinquent servant of a foreign ambassador," but reported that "the victim either really, or craftily, fell into a swoon and the experiment had to be discontinued." I can't say that I blame him.

Experiments continued throughout the 17th and 18th centuries but with mixed results. Part of the problem was the suitability of the substances injected, which, depending on the illness being treated, might include things like cinnamon or arsenic.

Another problem was a poor understanding of how the circulatory system works; the English physician William Harvey may have first described the system in 1628, but it was many years before his ideas were fully accepted. A general belief persisted that the effects of an injected drug stayed local to the point of injection and that the drug didn't travel around the body. It was also widely believed by medical practitioners that a person's "craving" for opiates was akin to the hunger we have for food, and that you could not become addicted to opium unless you swallowed it. Therefore, they were quite indiscriminate in injecting people for even minor ailments, thus creating new addicts by accident.

This particular belief was shared by Alexander Wood, a 19th-century president of the Royal College of Physicians in Edinburgh, who is credited with being the father of modern hypodermic syringe use. However, it was his contemporary Charles Hunter, a house surgeon at St George's Hospital, who first realised that drugs administered by intravenous injection do indeed circulate in the blood. He discovered this after he was forced to move an injection site due to the formation of an abscess but found that his patient still benefited from the pain relief administered.

What followed was "a period of sustained and acrimonious debate between Wood and Hunter" but, ultimately, the truth couldn't be argued with.

## Misuse of a Life-Saving Invention

The arrival of modern syringes undoubtedly saved lives but also led to a rapid growth in their popularity among drug abusers.

"In the early 20th century addicts were taking doses that were enormous by today's standards and mostly had overdose experiences when they accidentally hit a vein," writes Richard Pates in the 2008 book "Injecting Illicit Drugs." "But when narcotics started to become more difficult to obtain and the doses became smaller, communication in the drug subculture facilitated the diffusion of the intravenous technique. [Intravenous] injecting is more economical and the enjoyable rapid effect, or 'rush', contributed to the quick diffusion."

Some of the health issues surrounding IV drug abuse—particularly needle sharing or contamination—can be alleviated by the use of needle exchange schemes and with colour-coded syringes that prevent users mistaking which are theirs. Another solution is to introduce medically supervised injecting facilities (SIFs) or drug consumption rooms (DCRs). These now exist in at least eight different countries.

But, ultimately, the best way to prevent people from causing injury to themselves with intravenous injection is to get them to stop using needles altogether. And that means dealing with the underlying reasons why people use them, a situation beautifully summed up by the American writer Wendell Berry in his 2003 book "The Art of the Commonplace":

"People use drugs, legal and illegal, because their lives are intolerably painful or dull. They hate their work and find no rest in their leisure. They are estranged from their families and their neighbours. It should tell us something that in healthy societies drug use is celebrative, convivial, and occasional, whereas among us it is lonely, shameful, and addictive. We need drugs, apparently, because we have lost each other."

During my career as police officer I met a great many needle-using drug addicts. Some worked in the sex industry to maintain their habit. Some had taken to street robbery or shoplifting. Many were homeless or chaotic sleepers. A few had fallen from a great height, having lost well-paid jobs and their families. One or two were literally born with the craving as their mothers had been addicts during pregnancy.

I never once met a happy user.

# CHAPTER 4

# Should the Medical Use of Illicit Drugs Be Exempt from Legal Repercussions?

# Questions for Consideration in Developing Drug Policy

*Mark A. R. Kleiman, Jonathan P. Caulkins, Angela Hawken, and Beau Kilmer*

*Mark Kleiman is a professor of public policy at the NYU Marron Institute of Urban Management, where he leads the Crime and Justice program. Jon Caulkins has been on the Heinz College faculty since 1990. Angela Hawken, PhD, is a professor of public policy at the NYU Marron Institute of Urban Management and director of the Litmus program. Beau Kilmer is a senior policy researcher at the RAND Corporation, where he codirects the RAND Drug Policy Research Center.*

D rug abuse—of licit and illicit drugs alike—is a big medical and social problem and attracts a substantial amount of research attention. But the most attractive and most easily fundable research topics are not always those with the most to contribute to improved social outcomes. If the scientific effort paid more attention to the substantial opportunities for improved policies, its contribution to the public welfare might be greater.

The current research agenda around drug policy concentrates on the biology, psychology, and sociology of drugtaking and on the existing repertoire of drug-control interventions. But that repertoire has only limited capacity to shrink the damage that drug users do to themselves and others or the harms associated with drug dealing, drug enforcement, and drug-related incarceration; and the current research effort pays little attention to some innovative policies with substantial apparent promise of providing improved results.

At the same time, public opinion on marijuana has shifted so much that legalization has moved from the dreams of enthusiasts

"Eight Questions for Drug Policy Research," by Mark A. R. Kleiman, Jonathan P. Caulkins, Angela Hawken, and Beau Kilmer, University of Texas at Dallas, 2012. Reprinted by permission.

to the realm of practical possibility. Yet voters looking to science for guidance on the practicalities of legalization in various forms find little direct help.

All of this suggests the potential of a research effort less focused on current approaches and more attentive to alternatives.

The standard set of drug policies largely consists of:

- Prohibiting the production, sale, and possession of drugs
- Seizing illicit drugs
- Arresting and imprisoning dealers
- Preventing the diversion of pharmaceuticals to nonmedical use
- Persuading children not to begin drug use
- Offering treatment to people with drug-abuse disorders or imposing it on those whose behavior has brought them into conflict with the law
- Making alcohol and nicotine more expensive and harder to get with taxes and regulations
- Suspending the drivers' licenses of those who drive while drunk and threatening them with jail if they keep doing it

With respect to alcohol and tobacco, there is great room for improvement even within the existing policy repertoire for example, by raising taxes), even before more-innovaive approaches are considered. With respect to the currently illicit drugs, it is much harder to see how increasing or slightly modifying standard-issue efforts will measurably shrink the size of the problems.

The costs—fiscal, personal, and social—of keeping half a million drug offenders (mostly dealers) behind bars are suficiently great to raise the question of whether less comprehensive but more targeted drug enforcement might be the better course. Various forms of focused enforcement offer the promise of greatly reduced drug abuse, nondrug crime, and incarceration. These include testing and sanctions programs, interventions to shrink flagrant retail drug markets, collecive deterrence directed at violent drug-dealing organizaions, and drug-law enforcement aimed at deterring and incapacitating unusually violent individual dealers. Substanial increases in alcohol taxes might also greatly reduce abuse, as might developing more-effective treatments for stimulant abusers or improving the actual evidence base underlying the movement toward "evidence-based policies."

These opportunities and changes ought to influence the esearch agenda. Surely what we try to find out should bear some relationship to the practical choices we face. Below we list eight research questions that we think would be worth answering. We have selected them primarily for policy relevance rather than for purely scientific interest.

## How Responsive Is Drug Use to Changes in Price, Risk, Availability, and "Normalcy?"

The fundamental policy question concerning any drug is whether to make it legal or prohibited. Although the choice is not merely binary, a fairly sharp line divides the spectrum of options. A substance is legal if a large segment of he population can purchase and possess it for unsupervised "recreational" use, and if there are no restrictions on who can produce and sell the drug beyond licensing and routine regulations.

Accepting that binary simplification, the choice becomes what kind of problem one prefers. Use and use-related problems will be more prevalent if the substance is legal. Prohibition will reduce, not eliminate, use and abuse, but with three principal costs: black markets that can be violent and corrupting, enforcement costs that exceed those of regulating a legal market, and increased damage per unit of consumption among those who use despite the ban. (Total use related harm could go up or down depending on the extent to which the reduction in use offsets the increase in harmfulness per unit of use.)

The costs of prohibition are easier to observe than are its benefits in the form of averted use and use-related problems. In that sense, prohibition is like investments in prevention, such as improving roads; it's easier to identify the costs than to identify lives saved in accidents that did not happen.

We would like to know the long-run effect on consumption of changes in both price and the nonprice aspects of availability, including legal risks and stigma. There is now a literature estimating the price elasticity of demand for illegal drugs, but the estimates vary widely from one study to the next and many studies are based on surveys that may not give adequate weight to the heavy users who dominate consumption. Moreover, legalization would probably involve price declines that go far beyond the support of historical data.

Furthermore, as Mark Moore pointed out many years ago, the nonprice terms of availability, which he conceptualized as "search cost," may match price effects in terms of their impact on consumption. Yet those effects have never been quantitatively estimated for a change as profound as that from illegality to legality. The decision not to enforce laws against small cannabis transactions in the Netherlands did not cause an explosion in use; whether and how much it increased consumption and whether the establishment of retail shops mattered remain controversial questions.

This ignorance about the effect on consumption hamstrings attempts to be objective and analytical when discussing the question of whether to legalize any of the currently illicit drugs, and if so, under what conditions.

## How Responsive Is the Use of Drug Y to Changes in Policy Toward Drug X?

Polydrug use is the norm, particularly among frequent and compulsive users. (Most users do not fall in that category, but the minority who do account for the bulk of consumption and harms.) Therefore, "scoring" policy interventions by considering only effects on the target substance is potentially misleading.

For example, driving up the price of one drug, say cocaine, might reduce its use, but victory celebrations should be tempered if the reduction stemmed from users switching to methamphetamine or heroin. On the other hand, school based drug-prevention efforts may generate greater benefits through effects on alcohol and tobacco abuse than via their effects on illegal drug use. Comparing them to other drug-control interventions, such as mandatory minimum sentences for drug dealers, in terms of ability to control illegal drugs alone is a mistake; those school-based prevention interventions are not (just) illicit-drug–control programs.

But policy is largely made one substance at a time. Drugs are added to schedules of prohibited substances based on their potential for abuse and for use as medicine. Reformers clamor for evidence-based policies that rank individual drugs' harmfulness, as attempted recently by David Nutt, and ban only the most dangerous. Yet it makes little practical sense to allow powder cocaine while banning crack, because anyone with baking soda and a microwave oven can convert powder to crack.

Considerations of substitution or complementarity ought to arise in making policy toward some of the so-called designer drugs. Mephedrone looks relatively good if most of its users would otherwise have been abusing methamphetamine; it looks terrible if in fact it acts as a stepping stone to methamphetamine use. But no one knows which is the case.

Marijuana legalization is in play in a way it has not been since the 1970s. Various authors have produced social-welfare analyses of marijuana legalization, toting up the benefits of reduced enforcement costs and the costs of greater need for treatment, accounting for potential tax revenues and the like.

Yet the marijuana-specific gains and losses from legalization would be swamped by the uncertainties concerning its effects on alcohol consumption. The damage from alcohol is a large multiple of the damage from cannabis; thus a 10% change, up or down, in alcohol abuse could outweigh any changes in marijuana-related outcomes.

There is conflicting evidence as to whether marijuana and alcohol are complements or substitutes; no one can rule out even larger increases or decreases in alcohol use as a result of marijuana legalization, especially in the long run.

Marijuana legalization might also influence heavy use of cocaine or cigarette smoking. But again, no one knows whether that effect would be to drive cocaine or cigarette use up or down, let alone by how much. If doubling marijuana use led to even a 1% increase or decrease in tobacco use, it could produce 4,000 more or 4,000 fewer tobacco-related deaths per year, far more than the (quite small) number of deaths associated with marijuana.

This uncertainty makes it impossible to produce a solid benefit/cost analysis of marijuana legalization with existing data. That suggests both caution in drawing policy conclusions and aggressive efforts to learn more about cross-elasticities among drugs prone to abuse.

## Can We Stop Large Numbers of Drug-Involved Criminal Offenders from Using Illicit Drugs?

Many county, state, and federal initiatives target drug use among criminal offenders. Yet most do little to curtail drug use or crime. An exception is the drug courts process; some implementations of that idea have been shown to reduce drug use and other illegal behavior. Unfortunately, the resource intensity of drug courts limits their potential scope. The requirement that every participant must appear regularly before a judge for a status hearing means that a drug court judge can oversee fewer than 100 offenders at any time.

The HOPE approach to enforcing conditions of probation and parole, named after Hawaii's Opportunity Probation with Enforcement, offers the potential for reducing use among drug-involved offenders at a larger scale. Like drug courts, HOPE provides swift and certain sanctions for probation violations, including drug use. HOPE starts with a formal warning that any violation of probation conditions will lead to an immediate but brief stay in jail. Probationers are then subject to regular random drug testing: six times a month at first, diminishing in frequency with sustained compliance. A positive drug test leads to an immediate arrest and a brief jail stay (usually a few days but in some jurisdictions as little as a few hours in a holding cell). Probationers appear before the judge only if they have violated a rule; in contrast, a drug court judge participates in every status review. Thus HOPE sites can supervise large numbers of offenders; a single judge in Hawaii now supervises more than 2,000 HOPE probationers.

In a large randomized controlled trial (RCT), Hawaii's HOPE program greatly outperformed standard probation in reducing drug use, new crimes, and incarceration among a population of mostly methamphetamine-using felony probationers. A similar program in Tarrant County, Texas (encompassing Arlington and Fort Worth), appears to produce similar results, although this has not yet been verified by an RCT, as has a smaller-scale program (verified by an RCT) among parolees in Seattle. Reductions in drug use of 80%, in new arrests of 30 to 50%, and in days behind bars of 50% appear to be achievable at scale. The last result is the most striking; get-tough automatic-incarceration policies can reduce incarceration rather than increasing it, if the emphasis is on certainty and celerity rather than severity.

The Department of Justice is funding four additional RCTs; those results should help clarify how generalizable the HOPE outcomes are. But to date there has been no systematic experimentation to test how variations in program parameters lead to variations in results.

Hawaii's HOPE program uses two days in jail as its typical first sanction. Penalties escalate for repeated violations, and the 15% or so of participants who violate a fourth time face a choice between residential treatment and prison. No one is mandated to undergo treatment except after repeated failures. The results suggest that this is an effective design, but is it optimal? Would some sanction short of jail for the first violation—a curfew, home confinement, or community service—work as well? Are escalating penalties necessary and if so, what is the optimal pattern of escalation? Is there a subset of offenders who ought to be mandated to treatment immediately rather than waiting for failures to accumulate? Should cannabis be included in the list of drugs tested for, as it is in Hawaii, or excluded? How about synthetically produced cannabinoids (sold as "Spice") and cathinones (sold as "bath salts"), which require more complex and costly screening? Would adding other services to the mix improve outcomes? How can HOPE be integrated with existing treatment-diversion programs and drug courts? How can HOPE principles best be applied to parole, pretrial release, and juvenile offenders?

Answering these questions would require measuring the results of systematic variation in program conditions. There is no strong reason to think that the optimal program design will be the same in every jurisdiction or for every offender population. But it's time to move beyond the question "Does HOPE work?" to consider how to optimize the design of testing-and-sanctions programs.

## Can We Stop Alcohol-Abusing Criminal Offenders from Getting Drunk?

Under current law, state governments effectively give every adult a license to purchase and consume alcohol in unlimited quantities. Judges in some jurisdictions can temporarily revoke that license for those with an alcohol-related offense by prohibiting drinking and going to bars as conditions of bail or probation. However, because alcohol passes through the body quickly, a typical random-but-infrequent testing regiment would miss most violations, making the revocation toothless.

In 2005, South Dakota embraced an innovative approach to this problem, called 24/7 Sobriety. As a condition of bail, repeat drunk drivers who were ordered to abstain from alcohol were now subject to twice-a-day breathalyzer tests, every day. Those testing positive or missing the test were immediately subject to a short stay in jail, typically a night or two. What started as a five-county pilot program expanded throughout the state, and judges began applying the program to offenders with all types of alcohol-related criminal behavior, not just drunk driving. Some jurisdictions even started using continuous alcohol-monitoring bracelets, which can remotely test for alcohol consumption every 30 minutes. Approximately

20,000 South Dakotans have participated in 24/7—an astounding figure for a state with a population of 825,000.

The anecdotal evidence about the program is spectacular; fewer than 1% of the 4.8 million breathalyzer tests ordered since 2005 were failed or missed. That is not because the offenders have no interest in drinking. About half of the participants miss or fail at least one test, but very few do so more than once or twice. 24/7 is now up and running in other states, and will soon be operating in the United Kingdom. As of yet there are no peer-reviewed studies of 24/7, but preliminary results from a rigorous quasi-experimental evaluation suggest that the program did reduce repeat drunk driving in South Dakota. Furthermore, as with HOPE, there remains a need to better understand for whom the program works, how long the effects last, the mechanism(s) by which it works, and whether it can be effective in a more urban environment.

Programs such as HOPE and 24/7 can complement traditional treatment by providing "behavioral triage." Identifying which subset of substance abusers cannot stop drinking on their own, even under the threat of sanctions, allows the system to direct scarce treatment resources specifically to that minority.

Another way to take away someone's drinking license would be to require that bars and package stores card every would be to require that bars and package stores card every buyer and to issue modified driver's licenses with nondrinker markings on them to those convicted of alcohol-related crimes. This approach would probably face legal and political challenges, but that should not discourage serious analysis of the idea.

There is also strong evidence that increasing the excise tax on alcohol could reduce alcohol-related crime. Duke University economist Philip Cook estimates that doubling the federal tax, leading to a price increase of about 10%, would reduce violent crime and auto fatalities by about 3%, a striking saving in deaths for a relatively minor and easy-to-administer policy change. There is also evidence that formal treatment, both psychological and pharmacological, can yield improvements in outcomes for those who accept it.

## How Concentrated Is Hard-Drug Use Among Active Criminals?

Literally hundreds of substances have been prohibited, but the big three expensive drugs (sometimes called the "hard" drugs)—cocaine, including crack; heroin; and methamphetamine—account for most of the societal harm. The serious criminal activity and other harms associated with those substances are further highly concentrated among a minority of their users. Many people commit a little bit of crime or use hard drugs a handful of times, but relatively few make a habit of either one. Despite their relatively small numbers, those frequent users and their suppliers account for a large share of all drug-related crime and violence.

The populations overlap; an astonishing proportion of those committing income-generating crimes, such as robbery, as opposed to arson, are drug-dependent and/or intoxicated at the time of their offense, and a large proportion of frequent users of expensive drugs commit income-generating crime. Moreover, the two sets of behaviors are causally linked. Among people with drug problems who are also criminally active, criminal activity tends to rise and fall with drug consumption. Reductions in crime constitute a major benefit of providing drug treatment for the offender population, or of imposing HOPE-style community supervision.

Reducing drug use among active offenders could also shrink illicit drug markets, producing benefits everywhere, from inner-city neighborhoods wracked by flagrant drug dealing to source and transit countries such as Colombia and Mexico.

A back-of-the envelope calculation suggests the potential size of these effects. The National Survey on Drug Use and Health estimates users in the household population. The Arrestee Drug Abuse Monitoring Program measures the rate of active substance use among active offenders (by self-report and urinalysis). Two decades ago, an author of this article (Kleiman) and Chris Putala, then on the Senate Judiciary Committee staff, used the predecessors of those surveys to estimate that about three-quarters of all heavy (more than-weekly) cocaine users had been arrested for a nondrug felony in the previous year.

Applying the Pareto Law's rule of thumb that 80% of the volume of any activity is likely to be accounted for by about 20% of those who engage in it—true, for example, about the distribution of alcohol consumption—suggests that something like three-fifths of all the cocaine is used by people who get arrested in the course of a typical year and who are therefore likely to be on probation, parole, or pretrial release if not behind bars.

Combining that calculation with the result from HOPE that frequent testing with swift and certain sanctions can shrink (in the Hawaii case) methamphetamine use among heavily drug-involved felony probationers by 80%, suggests that total hard-drug volume might be reduced by something like 50% if HOPE-style supervision were applied to all heavy users of hard drugs under criminal-justice supervision. No known drug-enforcement program has any comparable capability to shrink illicit-market volumes.

By the same token, HOPE seems to reduce criminal activity, as measured by felony arrests, by 30 to 50%. If frequent offenders commit 80% of income-generating crime, and half of those frequent offenders also have serious harddrug problems, such a reduction in offending within that group could reduce total income-generating crime by approximately 15 to 20%, while also decreasing the number of jail and prison inmates.

The Kleiman and Putala estimate was necessarily crude because it was based on studies that weren't designed to measure the concentration of hard-drug use among offenders. Unfortunately, no one in the interim has attempted to refine that estimate with more precise methods (for example, stochastic-process modeling) or more recent data.

## What Is the Evidence for Evidence-Based Practices?

Many agencies now recommend (and some states and federal grant programs mandate) adoption of prevention and treatment programs that are evidence-based. But the move toward evidence-based practices has one serious limitation: the quality of the evidence base. It is important to ask what qualifies as evidence and who gets to produce it. Many programs are expanded and replicated on the basis of weak evidence. Study design matters. A review by George Mason University Criminologist David Weisburd and colleagues showed that the effect size of offender programs is negatively related to study quality: The more rigorous the study is, the smaller its reported effects.

Who does the evaluation can also make a difference. Texas A&M Epidemiologist Dennis Gorman found that evaluations authored by program developers report much larger effect sizes than those authored by independent researchers. Yet Benjamin Wright and colleagues reported that more than half of the substance-abuse programs targeting criminal-justice programs that were designated as evidence-based on the Substance Abuse and Mental Health Services Administration's (SAMHSA's) National Registry of Evidence Based Programs and Practices (NREPP) include the program developer as evaluator. Consequently, we may be spending large sums of money on ineffective programs. Many jurisdictions, secure in their illusory evidence base, could become complacent about searching for alternative programs that really do work.

We need to get better at identifying effective strategies and helping practitioners sort through the evidence. Requiring that publicly funded programs be evaluated and show improved outcomes using strong research designs—experimental designs where feasible, well-designed historical control strategies where experiments can't be done, and "intent-to-treat" analyses rather than cherry-picking success by studying program completers only—would cut the number of programs designated as promising or evidence-based by more than 75%. Not only would this relieve taxpayers of the burden of supporting ineffective programs, it would also help researchers identify more promising directions for future intervention research.

The potential for selection biases when studying drug involved people is substantial and thus makes experimental designs much more valuable. Small is key. It avoids expense, and equally important, it avoids champions with bruised egos. It is difficult to scale back a program once an agency becomes invested in the project. Small pilot evaluations that do show positive outcomes can then be replicated and expanded if the replications show similarly positive results.

## What Treats Stimulant Abuse?

Science can alleviate social problems not only by guiding policy but also by inventing better tools. The holy grail of such innovations would be a technology that addresses stimulant dependence.

The ubiquitous "treatment works" mantra masks a sharp disparity in technologies available for treating opiates (heroin and oxycodone) as opposed to stimulants (notably cocaine, crack, and meth). A variety of so-called opiate-substitute therapies (OSTs) exist that essentially substitute supervised use of legal, pure, and cheap opiates for unsupervised use of street opiates. Methadone is the first and best-known OST, but there are others. A number of countries even use clinically supplied heroin to substitute for street heroin.

OST stabilizes dependent individuals' chaotic lives, with positive effects on a wide range of life outcomes, such as increased employment and reduced criminality and rates of overdose. Sometimes stabilization is a first step toward abstinence, but for better and for worse the dominant thinking since the 1980s has been to view substitution therapy as an open-ended therapy, akin to insulin for diabetics. Either way, OST consistently fares very well in evaluations that quantify social benefits produced relative to program costs.

There is no comparable technology for treating stimulant dependence. This is not for lack of trying. The National Institute on Drug Abuse has invested hundreds of millions of dollars in the quest for pharmacotherapies for stimulants. Decades of work have produced many promising advances in basic science, but with comparatively little effect on clinical practice. The gap between opiate and stimulant treatment technologies matters more in the United States and the rest of the Western Hemisphere, where stimulants have a large market, than in the rest of the world, where opiates remain predominant.

There are two reactions to this zero-for-very-many batting average. One is to redouble efforts; after all, Edison tried a lot of filament materials before hitting on carbonized bamboo. The other is to give up on the quest for a chemical that can offset, undo, or modulate stimulants' effects in the brain and pursue other approaches. For example, immunotherapies are a fundamentally different technology inasmuch as the active introduced agent does not cross the blood-brain barrier. Rather, the antibodies act almost more like interdiction agents, but interdicting the drug molecules between ingestion and their crossing the blood-brain barrier rather than interdicting at the nation's border.

There is evidence from clinical trials showing that some cognitive-behavioral therapies can reduce stimulant consumption for some individuals. Contingency management also takes a behavioral rather than a chemical approach, essentially incentivizing dependent users to remain abstinent. The stunning finding is that, properly deployed, very small incentives (for example, vouchers for everyday items) can induce much greater behavioral change than can conventional treatment methods alone.

The ability of contingency management to reduce consumption, and the finding that even the heaviest users respond to price increases by consuming less, profoundly challenge conventional thinking about the meaning of addiction. They seem superficially at odds with the clear evidence that addiction is a brain disease with a physiological basis. Brain imaging studies let us see literally how chronic use changes the brain in ways that are not reversed by mere withdrawal of the drugs. So just as light simultaneously displays characteristics of a particle and a wave, so too addiction simultaneously has characteristics of a physiological disease and a behavior over which the person has (at least limited) control.

## What Reduces Drug-Market Violence?

Drug dealers can be very violent. Some use violence to settle disputes about territory or transactions; others use violence to climb the organizational ladder or intimidate witnesses or enforcement officials. Because many dealers have guns or have easy access to them, they also sometimes use these weapons to address conflicts that have nothing to do with drugs. Because the market tends to replace drug dealers who are incarcerated, there is little reason to think that routine drug-law enforcement can reduce violence; the opposite might even be true if greater enforcement pressure makes violence more advantageous to those most willing to use it.

That raises the question of whether drug-law enforcement can be designed specifically to reduce violence. One set of strategies toward this end is known as focused deterrence or pulling-levers policing. These approaches involve lawenforcement officials directly communicating a credible threat to violent individuals or groups, with the goal of reducing the violence level, even if the level of drug dealing or gang activity remains the same. Such interventions aim to tip situations from high-violence to low-violence equilibria by changing the actual and perceived probability of punishment; for example, by making violent drug dealing riskier, in enforcement terms, than less violent drug dealing.

The seminal effort was the Boston gun project Ceasefire, which focused on reducing juvenile homicides in the mid-1990s. Recognizing that many of the homicides stemmed from clashes between juvenile gangs, the strategy focused on telling members of each gang that if anyone in the gang shot someone (usually a member of a rival gang) police and prosecutors would pull every lever legally available against the entire gang, regardless of which individual had pulled the trigger. Instead of receiving praise from colleagues for increasing the group's prestige, the potential shooter now had to deal with the fact that killing put the entire group at risk. Thus the social power of the gang was enlisted on the side of violence reduction. The results were dramatic: Youth gun homicides in Boston fell from two a month before the intervention to zero while the intervention lasted. Variants of Ceasefire have been implemented across the country, some with impressive results.

An alternative to the Ceasefire group-focused strategy is a focus on specific drug markets where flagrant dealing leads to violence and disorder. Police and prosecutors in High Point, North Carolina, adopted a focused-deterrence approach, which involved strong collaborations with community members. Their model, referred to as the Drug Market Intervention, involved identifying all of the dealers in the targeted market, making undercover buys from them (often on film), arresting the most violent dealers, and not arresting the others. Instead, the latter were invited to a community meeting where they were told that, although cases were made against them, they were going to get another chance as long as they stopped dealing. The flagrant drug market in that neighborhood, as David Kennedy reports, vanished literally overnight and has not reappeared for the subsequent seven years. The program has been replicated in dozens of jurisdictions, and there is a growing evidence base showing that it can reduce crime.

A third approach recognizes the heterogeneity in violence among individual drug dealers. By focusing enforcement on those identified as the most violent, police can create both Darwinian and incentive pressures to reduce the overall violence level. This technique has yet to be systematically evaluated. This seems like an attractive research opportunity if a jurisdiction wants to try out such an approach.

An especially challenging problem is dealing-related violence in Mexico, now claiming more than 1,000 lives per month. It is worth considering whether a Ceasefire-style strategy might start a tipping process toward a less violent market. Such a strategy could exploit two features of the current situation: The Mexican groups make most of their money selling drugs for distribution in the United States, and the United States has much greater drug enforcement capacity than does Mexico. If the Mexican government were to select one of the major organizations and target it for destruction after a transparent process based on relative violence levels, US drug-law enforcement might be able to put the target group out of business by focusing attention on the US distributors that buy their drugs from the target Mexican organization, thereby pressuring them to find an alternative source. If that happened, the target organization would find itself without a market for its product.

If one organization could be destroyed in this fashion, the remaining groups might respond to an announcement that a second selection process was underway by competitively reducing their violence levels, each hoping that one of its rivals would be chosen as the second target. The result might be—with the emphasis on might—a dramatic reduction in bloodshed.

Whatever the technical details of violence-minimizing drug-law enforcement, its conceptual basis is the understanding that in established markets enforcement pressure can have a greater effect on how drugs are sold than on how much is sold. So violence reduction is potentially more feasible than is greatly reducing drug dealing generally.

## Conclusion

Drug policy involves contested questions of value as well as of fact; that limits the proper role of science in policymaking. And many of the factual questions are too hard to be solved with the current state of the art: The mechanisms of price and quantity determination in illicit markets, for example, have remained largely impervious to investigation. Conversely, research on drug abuse can provide insight into a variety of scientifically interesting questions about the nature of human motivation and self-regulation, complicated by imperfect information, intoxication, and impairment, and engaging group dynamics and tipping phenomena; not every study needs to be justified in terms of its potential contribution to making better policy. However, good theory is often developed in response to practical challenges, and policymakers need the guidance of scientists. Broadening the current research agenda away from biomedical studies and evaluations of the existing policy repertoire could produce both more interesting science and more successful policies.

# Can Employees Smoke Marijuana on the Job?

## The Emplawyerologist Firm

*The Law Office of Janette Levey Frisch—also referred to as the "EmpLAWyerologist" Firm—focuses on the rights of employers. Its priority is minimizing employers' exposure to liability from litigation and audits and helping employers improve employer-employee relations. They have a blog of the same name related to these issues.*

D o you conduct pre-employment drug screens? What if one of your applicants tests positive for marijuana? What if that candidate presents you with a card, showing that s/he uses medical marijuana, for treatment of a chronic condition? As you may know, medical marijuana is legal in at least 24 states, and the District of Columbia. Some state courts have also ruled that you cannot fire or refuse to hire an applicant/employee just because s/he uses medical marijuana. What if you employ people in one or more of those states? Can you still conduct drug screening? Can you still enforce drug-free workplace policies or does that all go to pot? (Sorry I just couldn't resist). Read on to learn what you can and cannot do, and what you may or may not have to do.

First, don't scrap your drug testing or drug-free workplace policies so fast. Yes, more than half the States have legalized medical marijuana. In most cases, all that really means is that someone who does use marijuana for medicinal purposes is protected from criminal prosecution for marijuana use/possession. By and large these statutes are silent on any employment issues that medical marijuana may raise. Furthermore, marijuana use and possession is still a federal crime, and federal officials and agencies still take the position that medical marijuana users are not protected from criminal prosecution—at least not under federal law.

"Holy Smoke! Do You Have to Allow Medical Marijuana at Work?" by The Emplawyerologist Firm, July 20, 2017. Reprinted by permission.

Some states have started passing legislation and some state courts have issued some rulings that go beyond the issue of criminal prosecution. Let's have a look. Pennsylvania recently passed a law expressly prohibiting employers from discriminating against candidates or employees based on their status as medical marijuana card holders. However, that law only speaks to the issue of positive drug test results, and only then with respect to very specific duties (e.g. public utility workers). New Jersey's medical marijuana law states that employers do not have to accommodate medical marijuana use at work, but says nothing about after-hours use. Arizona, Minnesota and Delaware provide specific protection to employees with medical authorization who test positive for marijuana. The Supreme Judicial Court of Massachusetts just issued a ruling that an employee fired for medical marijuana use (which showed up on a drug test) could file a disability discrimination suit under state law.

What do you do if you employ people in any of the above states? At a minimum, you would have to look past the positive test results. You might then need to determine if there are any jobs at your company for which a positive test result would be an issue. Such jobs could certainly include safety-sensitive positions. You would probably want to document any jobs where you believe the positive test result is an issue. You may need to show that the employee is impaired during work hours due to his or her marijuana use. Unfortunately, neither these laws nor the courts in those states tend to provide guidance as to how to make that determination. (Urine tests do not measure impairment.)

What about the Americans with Disabilities Act? Wouldn't it provide protection here? Would allowing the use of medical marijuana be a reasonable accommodation? As of now, no federal court has taken that position, and probably will not do so as long as marijuana use/possession remains a federal crime. (NOTE: Last year, the US Supreme Court refused to hear a case asking for legalization of medical marijuana.) That does not mean that you would not have to provide some *other* reasonable accommodation for the employee with respect to the underlying condition. It just means that you are not required under the Americans with Disabilities Act to alter a drug-free workplace policy, whether or not the employee has medical authorization to use marijuana.

While it would seem clear that you can prohibit employees from using or being under the influence of medical marijuana *during* work hours, what about after hours? The answer to that question is also unclear. Neither the US Supreme Court nor federal circuit courts have ruled that allowing after hour use can never be a reasonable accommodation. In fact, there is a pending case in New Jersey on that issue. A temporary employee, who disclosed his medical marijuana use to the staffing agency up front, initially was hired with no issues–until he was up for a new assignment that required a drug test. In the wake of the positive test result, he was terminated, and he sued, alleging disability discrimination under the New Jersey Law Against Discrimination. The staffing agency moved to dismiss, arguing that since marijuana use is illegal under federal law, it cannot be a reasonable accommodation. The employee argued that the NJLAD is supposed to be construed broadly to provide protection to disabled people, which should include medical marijuana users. The court has yet to decide this case, so stay tuned. (The case is *Barrett v Robert Half Corp.*)

OK, you may be thinking, can we cut to the chase? Can we test for drugs? Can we enforce zero-tolerance drug policies? Must we accommodate medical marijuana or not? In most states I would say yes, you can enforce those zero-tolerance policies, and no you do not have to hire someone who tests positive for marijuana. In the states mentioned above, however, you should proceed with caution—which of course means, check with local employment counsel, and look at whether and when such use might negatively impact an employee's to perform their job functions safely.

This seems like a good place to stop for now—so I will, until next week, or course. See you then.

Contents of this post are for educational/informational purposes only, are not legal advice, and do not create an attorney-client relationship. Consult with competent employment counsel in the state(s) in which you employ people with your specific questions.

# Legalizing Cannabis Could Have Positive Benefits

*Teri Moore*

*Teri Moore is a policy analyst and editor at the Reason Foundation. The Reason Foundation works on developing, applying, and promoting libertarian principles including individual liberty, free markets, and the rule of law.*

The US has spent over a trillion dollars during four decades on the "War on Drugs," with little to show for it. That "war" has sought to eliminate certain drugs rather than the harms associated with them (such as addiction, overdoses, and harmful acts perpetrated by drug users). Ironically, many of these harms have been partially mitigated at surprisingly low costs—not by the ill-conceived War on Drugs, but by ending the war on one drug, marijuana. Legalizing marijuana is reducing the social harms related to drug use by exerting its own pincer movement through simple supply and demand.

## Demand

Proponents of the War on Drugs have the "opioid crisis" in their sights. According to a report by the Council of Economic Advisors, opioid use cost US taxpayers about $500 billion in 2015, primarily as a result of additional health care expenditures and losses in productivity, on top of the $8 billion spent on criminal justice enforcement.

It's difficult to measure the extent of opioid use—and therefore demand—because so much of it is illegal. Illegal use is typically observed primarily through the arrest, death or hospitalization of users. If those statistics increase sharply (which they have), we can

"Marijuana Legalization Can Help Solve the Opioid Problem," by Teri Moore, Reason, April 3, 2018. Reprinted by permission.

assume that use has increased, but such metrics do not capture the actual extent of use.

But while demand for opioids seems to have risen, the rate of increase has been higher in some places than others. In particular, in places where medical cannabis is legal, marijuana has likely at least partially displaced opioids.

Canada has had a comprehensive national program of legalized medical cannabis since 2014. A recent University of British Columbia patient survey found 63 percent of Canadian opioid prescription drug patients had substituted cannabis for prescription drugs, 30 percent of which were for opioids. These patients cited fewer side effects, less addictivity and better symptom management.

In the states where it's legal, medical marijuana is likely serving the same purpose for many US opioid users. Twenty-nine states and the District of Columbia have legalized medical marijuana. A 2014 study found that in states that had legalized medical marijuana between 1999 and 2010, the incidence of opioid mortality was lower than in states where marijuana was not legalized for medical purposes. Meanwhile, a more recent study found that medical marijuana legalization was associated on average with 23 percent fewer opioid-related hospitalizations.

Opioids are powerful analgesics and as such have substantial benefits for pain management. However, opioid users may have trouble gauging safe dosage, especially when they are unaware of the actual dose of the opioid they are taking—a common problem with opioids purchased illegally. But they don't have that problem if they switch to marijuana, which has no known lethal dose. According to the National Cancer Institute, "Because cannabinoid receptors, unlike opioid receptors, are not located in the brainstem areas controlling respiration, lethal overdoses from *Cannabis* and cannabinoids do not occur." For those opioid users who have become addicted to opioids, substituting a drug that is not physically addictive and has no known lethal dose can only be a positive step.

While legalized medical marijuana results in relatively fewer opioid deaths, legalizing marijuana for recreational use seems to have resulted in an absolute reduction in such deaths. A 2017 study published in the *American Journal of Public Health* found that opioid mortality rates in Colorado fell following the legalization of recreational marijuana, reversing an upward trend in opioid deaths.

The stated preference of many opioid users for marijuana, combined with lower opioid hospitalization and mortality, means legalized marijuana likely correlates to a lower demand for opioids and a higher demand for marijuana.

## Supply

Over time, the price of recreational marijuana in Colorado and Washington has fallen. That's because legalization, when it's done right, drives competition and that drives innovation, leading to more efficient production and distribution. Ideally, prices fall below black market rates, thereby supplanting the black market created by prohibition.

Illegal substances are more risky to produce, transport and sell because every party faces the possibility of criminal sanction. Moreover, the inability to enforce agreements legally means that enforcement typically comes by way of a gun. So the prices of illegal substances tend to be higher than their legal equivalents—to compensate parties for the additional risks they face and because illegal markets tend to be subject to local monopolies. This results in a cascade of unintended, harmful consequences to society. Full legalization removes these risks to producers, sellers and users, thereby eliminating the associated violence and related social harms.

## Ending the War on Drugs and Winning the War on Social Harms from Drugs

Legalization of marijuana would bring transparency to business transactions and address many goals that the War on Drugs has failed so miserably to achieve:

- *Reduced harmful drug use:* With legal options, both recreational and therapeutic drug users are less likely to use and become addicted to more-dangerous substances, as found above with opioids.
- *Decreased overdose mortality:* According to the American Society of Addiction Medicine, "Drug overdose is the leading cause of accidental death in the US, with 52,404 lethal drug overdoses in 2015. Opioid addiction is driving this epidemic, with 20,101 overdose deaths related to prescription pain relievers, and 12,990 overdose deaths related to heroin in 2015." When legal or illegal opioid use is displaced by legal marijuana use, overdose mortality declines, as found in Colorado. And it does so at no cost to the taxpayer (indeed, since legal weed is taxed, it actually generates revenue). As such, it is a highly cost-effective way to address this tragic problem.

Mortality from illegal opioids is typically due to overdose. That can be simply the result of a mistake on the part of an addict. But it is often caused or exacerbated by drugs that do not contain what vendors claim they contain. Often fentanyl is cut into or sold as heroin. With fentanyl's vastly lower lethal dose, heroin users are more likely to overdose.

Tainted drugs also play a part. Sellers can derive greater profits when cutting heroin or fentanyl with visually similar substances, such as laundry detergent and strychnine. Opioid users who substitute marijuana also run the risk of tainted product in states where marijuana is illegal. Illegal marijuana is sometimes moistened with water or even Windex as a means of increasing weight or volume and masking the smell of mold.

But with legalization comes known supply chains, reputation and liability (customers can sue if they are sold a tainted product). That means cannabis bought legally is far less likely to be cut with unknown and possibly toxic substances, or let to mold. Customers of legalized marijuana can know the strength of what they're buying, unlike buying in the black market, which means a more informed consumer who can make better choices about product and dose.

- *Reduced drug-related incarceration rates:* By definition, legalization brings a lower incarceration rate, but that's not the goal here. After all, legalizing murder would cause the homicide incarceration rate to plummet! An incarcerated murderer is less likely to murder others. But when a substance that is far less lethal than alcohol is banned, arguably justice is out of whack and incarceration is uncalled for. The ACLU found that in 2010 American police arrested more people for (typically small amounts of) marijuana than for all other illegal drugs combined. This has cost taxpayers billions of dollars and has inflicted pain on many young lives unnecessarily and unfairly, and not only through incarceration. Merely having an arrest record prevents many from gainful and productive employment. Legalization rectifies this imbalance of justice, relieves overwhelmed prisons, and does not arbitrarily favor alcohol over marijuana.
- *Reduced dangerous drug availability:* We've learned through the failed War on Drugs that availability (supply) cannot be legislated away. The only effective recourse is lowered demand. While demand for marijuana has increased in states where it is legal, it appears to be displacing use for more-dangerous drugs—a welcome trade-off.
- *Reduced social harms:* With marijuana legalization cutting the black market price, drug cartels have had to abandon marijuana trafficking in favor of heroin and other opioids that can still turn a profit on the black market. With a reduced share of the market comes reduced illicit drug activity and all

the social harm it engenders, such as rampant theft and other property crime, street violence, territorial shootings and other gang-related illicit drug activity. This decreases violence, which often spills over into mainstream society, especially in places with high illicit drug use and trafficking.

Marijuana legalization is chipping away at the social and personal harms of dangerous drug use more effectively and vastly less expensively than the failed War on Drugs. While it's less offensive to blame other nations than ourselves, interdiction doesn't lessen demand for illegal drugs in this country: it makes them scarce and expensive, and drives a host of black market, underground, violent criminal enterprises. Moreover, it costs billions of dollars that could be used for other more socially useful purposes, including prevention and treatment of addiction. Conversely, marijuana legalization moves transactions into legal markets, allowing a vastly safer alternative for recreational and medical opioid users.

In economics 101, students learn about the "laws" of supply and demand. The War on Drugs has been waged in ignorance of this lesson. Legalization of marijuana shows that those laws still prevail and can be used to win the war on social harms from drugs.

# Misuse and Abuse of Legal Stimulants Requires Analysis and New Policy

*Steve Sussman, Mary Ann Pentz, Donna Spruijt-Metz, and Toby Miller*

*Steve Sussman and Mary Ann Pentz are professors of preventative medicine in the Keck School of Medicine at USC. Donna Spruijt-Metz is director of the USC mHealth Collaboratory at the University of Southern California's Center for Economic and Social Research and a professor of research in psychology and preventative medicine. Toby Miller is currently a research professor of the graduate division at University of California, Riverside, and president of the Cultural Studies Association.*

Prescription stimulants that have been used non-medically/illegally often have been referred to as "study drugs" or "cramming drugs," and sometimes "kiddy coke." Methylphenidate (e.g., Ritalin) is the most widely misused and researched of these drugs and has been referred to as "Vitamin R," "Skippy," "the Smart Drug," "Smarties," "Poor Man's Cocaine," "West Coast," and "R Ball." While prescribed for sufferers of Attention-Deficit/Hyperactivity Disorder (ADHD), and costing approximately $0.50 a pill when obtained licitly, prescription stimulant pills can cost $3 to $15 each when sold illicitly. Several recent news articles have been published about potential dangers of misuse of study drugs, and in February 2006, a Food and Drug Administration advisory panel urged that the strongest possible safety warning (the "black box" warning for cardiac problems and sudden death in pediatric patients) be used on these drugs. This review will describe briefly the history of prescription stimulants, their prevalence of misuse

"Misuse of 'Study Drugs': Prevalence, Consequences, and Implications for Policy," by Steve Sussman, Mary Ann Pentz, Donna Spruijt-Metz, and Toby Miller, BioMed Central Ltd, June 9, 2006. Reprinted by permission.

among emerging adults, and potential negative consequences. Policy implications also will be suggested.

## Brief History and Current Status of Study Drugs

Methylphenidate was first created in 1944 as part of a search for a non-addictive stimulant, and it was suggested as a means of regulating children's behavior in 1963, to control "hyperkinesis." Eventually such problematic behavior among children became labeled as "Attention-Deficit/Hyperactivity Disorder" (ADHD). ADHD refers to a constellation of dysfunctions that hinder attention regulation, motor behavior, impulsivity, emotional expression, and planning.

By 1970, 15 different pharmaceutical companies manufactured over 30 kinds of prescription stimulant-type products. Eventually a very large ADHD drug market developed, which has been dominated by stimulants. These currently include methylphenidate (brand names: Ritalin, Ritalin SR, Methylin, Methylin ER, Metadate, Metadate ER, Concerta), demethylphenidate (brand name: Focalin) and amphetamine preparations including D-amphetamine (brand names: Dexedrine, Spansule, Dextrostat), methamphetamine (brand name: Desoxyn) and D, L-amphetamine (brand names: Adderall, Adderall XL). People have observed the misuse of study drugs among those not diagnosed with ADHD, particularly among emerging adults. "Emerging adulthood" is a recently "coined" developmental period, referring to young people 18–25 years of age, who bridge the gap between adolescence and young adulthood. Misuse has been observed particularly in college settings. Many misuse these drugs to help keep alert and concentrate as they prepare ("cram") for tests or complete term papers (though, of course, people may misuse them for a variety of reasons)—hence the term "study drugs."

## Prevalence of Non-Medical Use of Prescription Stimulants: College Settings

Regarding college prevalence data and policy, the most frequently studied prescription stimulant is methylphenidate. From 1990 to 2000, use of methylphenidate increased five-fold in the United States, which consumes approximately 90% of all methylphenidate. The Monitoring the Future research group has been studying the annual prevalence of use of methylphenidate (measured as "Ritalin," as a stand-alone question) among teens and emerging adults since 2001. The annual prevalence among 8th, 10th, and 12th graders has averaged 2.7%, 4.3%, and 4.5%, respectively, over the period from 2001 to 2004. Its use among college students has averaged 5.0% over this period, whereas its use among non-college emerging adults has averaged approximately 2.9% over this period. (About 25% of these users use methylphenidate about once a month.)

Its use remains at approximately 3.5% through 24 years age. At 25 years of age its use decreases to 1.5% and then below 1% at 29–30 years of age. Thus, use of this study drug appears to peak from the ages of 16 to 24 years of age (older adolescence through emerging adulthood), following the same course of use prevalence as other drugs such as alcohol and illicit drugs. Males are relatively likely to use methylphenidate (3.7% versus 1.6%), and use appears slightly higher in the southern states in the Monitoring the Future survey (2.8% versus 2.0–2.5%), and in very large urban areas (about 3.0% versus 1.9–2.7%). Methylphenidate appears most likely to be used by male college students in large cities.

Several studies have been completed to discern prevalence and reasons for non-medical use of prescription stimulants. Simoni-Wastila & Strickler examined 1991–1993 data from the National Household survey on Drug Abuse (NHSDA), a nationally representative, randomized-block selected household sample of 12-year olds and older. They found that 1% of the US population had used prescription stimulants non-medically in the past year, and a fifth of them reported problem use (e.g., inability to cut down use), though they failed to find significant demographic, health status, or drug use correlates of illicit problem stimulant use. Certainly, the age range of highest lifetime use of prescription stimulants is from 18–25, approximately 5%, and at least doubling percentage figures among other age categories viewed across multiple years of this survey.

In a more recent study, McCabe and colleagues examined the prevalence rates and correlates of non-medical use of prescription stimulants (methylphenidate, D-amphetamine, or D,L-amphetamine) among US college students. One hundred and nineteen nationally representative 4-year colleges in the United States were selected and a sample of 10,904 randomly selected college students in 2001 were examined via self-report surveys. The life-time prevalence of non-medical prescription stimulant use was 6.9%, past year prevalence was 4.1% (but ranged from 0% to 25% across colleges), and past month prevalence was 2.1%. A total of 5.8% of males and 2.9% of females reported annual use of non-prescribed stimulants. In addition, 2.8% of males (1.6% of females) reported use in the past month. Whites were relatively likely to misuse prescription stimulants compared to African American, Asian, or other groups (annual use: 4.9% versus 1.6%, 1.3%, and 3.1%, respectively). The prevalence of non-medical use of prescription stimulants among students attending historically African American colleges and universities was low.

Past year rates of non-medical use ranged from zero to 25% at individual colleges. Non-medical use was higher among college students who were members of fraternities and sororities (annual use: 13.3% if living in a fraternity or sorority house, 3.5%-4.5% otherwise; 8.0% versus 1.8%–2.5% last month use), and earned lower grade point averages (annual use: B or lower average, 5.2%; B+ or higher, 3.3%). Rates were higher at colleges located in the north-eastern region of the U.S. (6.3% annual use), and southern region (4.6%), then other regions (2.8–3.2%), and colleges with more competitive admission standards (5.9% versus 1.3–4.5% annual use). Non-medical prescription stimulant users were more likely to report use of alcohol, cigarettes, marijuana, ecstasy, and cocaine, raising the possibility that use of prescription stimulants for non-medical purposes may be related as much to an addiction disorder as to an aid to study.

These studies examined a variety of prescription stimulant drugs, not just methylphenidate. Thus, arguably, a 4.1–5.4% annual prevalence represents the most accurate statement regarding those at highest prevalence of non-prescription use.

Several single-university sample surveys of college students have reported a range of use reports. Massachusetts, Michigan, New Hampshire, Maine, Florida, Pennsylvania, Wisconsin, and Texas samples are reported herein. In one random sample at a Massachusetts college of liberal arts (n = 283), 16.6% of the sample reported having taken methylphenidate for fun (non-medical purposes), and 12.7% reported having snorted methylphenidate; a majority of the self-reported users were under 24 years of age.

Teter, McCabe and colleagues administered a survey to 2250 randomly selected undergraduates at the University of Michigan (in 2001) and found a 3% annual prevalence of illicit methylphenidate use, which was positively associated with other licit and illicit drug use (but not with gender or ethnicity). The same research group assessed the prevalence and motives for illicit use of prescription stimulants (methylphenidate [two brands], D-amphetamine, and D, L-amphetamine) to a random sample of 9,161 undergraduate college students at the University of Michigan (surveyed in 2003). Of the study participants, 8.1% reported lifetime and 5.4% reported past-year illicit use of prescription stimulants. The most prevalent motives given for illicit use of prescription stimulants were to (1) help with concentration (58% of lifetime illicit users), (2) increase alertness (43%), and (3) provide a high (43%). Eighty-six percent reported not being prescribed these drugs in their lifetime. Men were more likely than women to report illicit use of prescription stimulants (9.3% versus 7.2%), and Whites and Hispanics (9.5% and 8.9%, respectively) were more likely to use them than African American or Asian students (2.7% and 4.9%, respectively). Illicit use of prescription stimulants was associated with elevated rates of alcohol and other drug use, and total number of motives endorsed and alcohol and other drug use were positively associated.

These same authors reported an additional study of prescription drug misuse and diversion (i.e., diverting use from those prescribed the medication to those not prescribed the medication), in the same cohort as the Teter et al. study. The annual illicit use of stimulant medication was 5%, and the illicit use-medical use ratio for stimulant medication (overall = 2.45) was the highest among the four classes of prescription drugs examined (overall ratios for the other three drug types, sleeping, sedative/anxiety, and pain medications were less than 1.0). Medical users of stimulants for attention deficit hyperactivity disorder were the most likely to be approached to divert their medication (54% of them reported being approached to sell, trade, or give away their medication). Illicit users of medical stimulants were relatively likely to use other drugs (odds ratios varied from 6.00 for binge drinking to 21.25 for annual cocaine use).

White, Becker-Blease, & Grace-Bishopexamined illicit use of stimulant medication among undergraduate and graduate students at the University of New Hampshire. Of 1,025 randomly sampled participants, 16% reported misusing stimulant medication (96% of those that specified a medication preferred to misuse methylphenidate, 2% misused D, L-amphetamine). Ninety-percent of these subjects reported never receiving an ADHD diagnosis. Results failed to differ as a function of gender. Most used pill form (55%), but 40% had used intranasally. Of those that misused prescription stimulants, about 50% reported misuse 2–3 per year, whereas the other 50% reported misuse at least once per month. Reasons for misusing prescription stimulant medication (i.e., illegal use) included improving attention, partying, reducing hyperactivity, and improving grades.

In a convenience sample survey of 150 undergraduates at a small US college (in Maine), 35.5% took prescription amphetamines (D,L-amphetamine, methylphenidate, or D-amphetamine) illegally. A total of 24% of the illicit users used amphetamines to study, but 19.3% used them in combination with alcohol for recreational reasons.

There have been several unpublished surveys conducted by individual colleges. For example, Kapner summarized four unpublished surveys of methylphenidate use from college reports, and found that 1.5% of students surveyed at the University of Florida in 2002 reported using methylphenidate recreationally in the last 30 days, 9% of those undergraduates surveyed at the University of Pennsylvania in 2000 had used someone else's ADHD prescription medication, 20% of those students surveyed at the University of Wisconsin, Madison, in 1998, had illegally taken an ADHD medication at least once, and 2% and 1.5% of those students surveyed at the University of Texas in 1997 had used methylphenidate illegally in their lifetimes and the past year, respectively. The sampling details of these reports were not disclosed and could not be located; thus, these results must be taken with caution. In the studies involving college students, college student participation rates among those "randomly" selected varied from 20–60%. Thus, replication studies with recruitment of a greater percentage of the targeted sample still are needed, if this can be accomplished in college settings.

To summarize, lifetime, past year, and past month illicit use of prescription stimulants among emerging adults appears to vary widely while averaging approximately 7%, 4%, and 2%, nationally. Use is most prevalent among white or Hispanic male college students, who are associated with fraternities, struggling with their grades, and who generally live in larger urban areas (though not always) in northeastern or southern regions of the U.S. These youth also tend to use other drugs particularly cannabis, alcohol, MDMA, and cocaine. They use study drugs to enhance their study and social life, and sometimes to stay awake while using another drug such as alcohol.

### Routes of Administration

Prescription stimulants have been misused through oral, intranasal, and intravenous routes of administration. Oral misuse of prescription stimulants results in noticeable symptoms if taken in high doses. Encapsulated extended-release formulas can be misused and abused as well as the older shorter-release formulas by breaking open a capsule and snorting the contents. A series of case studies have indicated intranasal and injection abuse of study drugs. In one study of New Hampshire undergraduate and graduate students, the preferred method of use among study drug misusers was oral (55%), intranasal (40%), and "Other" (4%). The route of administration of the "other" category was not specified, but it is possible that intravenous use was being referred to. More disconcerting, 79% of illicit users were not at all concerned about using these study drugs.

## Potential Negative Consequences of "Study Drug" Use

There are three general potential negative consequences of misusing study drugs. These include: (a) potential for addiction, (b) potential for reactions to high doses, (c) and potential for medical complications. These three consequences are discussed next.

### Addiction

A review of 60 studies suggested that the reinforcing or subjective effects of methylphenidate (in 80% of these studies) functions similarly to d-amphetamine or cocaine (i.e., as a reinforcer, in drug discrimination substitution, and subjective effects such as producing a "high" or "rush"), and that there is definite abuse potential. Tolerance develops and characteristic stimulant withdrawal symptoms have been reported including fatigue or exhaustion, depression, unpleasant and vivid dreams, insomnia or hypersomnia, increased appetite, psychomotor retardation or agitation, or irritability. Similar effects may be expected with all prescription stimulants.

Stimulants tend to increase or augment dopaminergic (reward, anticipation) and serotoninergic (self-administration initiation, maintenance of pleasure) neurotransmission. Methylphenidate appears to work by blocking pre-synaptic dopaminergic transporters, and does not appear to affect the serotonergic system. Its effects on dopaminergic transmission are similar to cocaine, and may lead to similar consequences through intranasal administration or injection. For example, in 23 case studies of intravenous methylphenidate use, the pattern of withdrawal and toxicity symptoms were similar to that of cocaine and amphetamine.

Oral use produces its effect in approximately an hour compared to a couple of minutes for other routes of methylphenidate (or cocaine) administration. Oral intake does not produce nearly as much reinforcing effect and, hence, has much less abuse potential, depending on the dose taken. Still, one should not stop using oral methylphenidate abruptly if one has been using it consistently, because it will produce withdrawal symptoms characteristic of other stimulants. Much more work is needed on the study of how routes of administration may interface with misuse and addiction to prescription stimulants.

### High Doses

At high doses, study drugs can produce symptoms such as emotional lability, anxiety, twitchiness, aggressiveness, loss of appetite, confusion, dizziness or blurred vision, insomnia, headaches, sweating, and dryness of the mouth and eyes. Methylphenidate and other study drug misuse may result in formification hallucinations (e.g., one may have a tactile perception as if there are bugs under ones skin), repetitive behaviors ("tweaking"), and bizarre delusions (e.g., personalization of objects, paranoia), if used chronically at high doses, especially by intranasal administration or injection.

In 1990, there were about 271 emergency room reports involving methylphenidate, 1,727 in 1998, and 1,478 in 2001. The total number of emergency department visits resulting from use of all psychotherapeutic CNS stimulants was 4091 in 1998,

3644 in 1999, 3336, in 2000, 3146 in 2001 and 3275 in 2002. There are approximately 25 emergency room deaths per year among up to 3 million users of prescription stimulant drugs (including both those medically prescribed and not prescribed these drugs). Thus, the likelihood of dying from such drugs appears to be approximately 1 in 120,000.

## Medical Complications

Most study drugs raise blood pressure and may place users at risk for heart attacks and stroke. For example, side effects may include irregular heartbeat and very high blood pressure. Thus, use is contraindicated if one has a history of high blood pressure or other cardiovascular-related concerns. In addition, use is contraindicated among those suffering from psychiatric conditions including severe anxiety, glaucoma, motor tics (or Tourette's syndrome), psychotic conditions, depression, a seizure disorder, or a history of drug abuse. Also, one should not use prescription stimulants if one has experienced a narrowing of ones gastrointestinal tract or a damaged liver. Finally, use also is contraindicated if one is taking other prescribed drugs particularly monoamine oxidase (MAO) inhibitors.

Intravenous use of prescription stimulants is particularly dangerous. In particular, intravenous (IV) abuse of methylphenidate may result in talcosis. Talcosis is a reaction to talc, a filler and lubricant in methylphenidate and other oral medication. This inflammation reaction occurs in the lungs and related consequences include lower lobe panacinar emphysema.

## Implications for Policy Change

Current rates of study drug misuse show the potential to increase dramatically in direct proportion to the prevalence of manufacture, prescription, and general availability. Five types of policy change are recommended to curb the misuse of these drugs.

First, limiting access to prescription stimulants may be a very important approach. Those who are correctly prescribed

ADHD medications could be involved in a monitoring system to try to make sure that they are not serving as suppliers to others. Fortunately, 21 states in the US use some sort of prescription monitoring program (PMP) to monitor the use of abuse-able prescription drugs. All these states include Schedule II stimulants as one of the drug categories being monitored and, often, lower scheduled ones as well.

Second, facilitating development of more safe alternative types of drugs may be very important as well. There is a relatively novel drug, Lilly's atomoxetine (brand name: Strattera), which has the advantage of not being classed as a central nervous system stimulant. Atomoxetine is a norepinephrine transporter inhibitor. It has similar side effects as the other drugs as well as potentially leading to urinary hesitation or retention. However, it probably has less abuse potential. There also exist novel pharmaceutical delivery systems that have been shown to be less prone to abuse (e.g., the Concerta formulation of methylphenidate). Possibly, use of these types of prescription drugs by those suffering from ADHD may lead to decreased prevalence of prescription drug misuse through diversion to those not suffering from ADHD. A recent study indicates very little misuse of the extended-release formula of methylphenidate in 2002.

The third change pertains to policies aimed at interdiction. These policies would be enforced by local law enforcement personnel to disrupt unauthorized points-of-sale or distribution. However, according to an article by Pentz and colleagues based on a review of interdiction policies aimed at other drugs, this type of policy has appeared to be largely ineffective.

The fourth is policies aimed at warning the public as well as users about the negative consequences of illicit use of prescription stimulants (study drugs). The FDA while having declared most of these drugs as controlled substances, should provide a wider array and more visible platforms (e.g., on labels, public announcements) discouraging misuse and highlighting negative consequences of use, unauthorized sales, and distribution of these drugs.

The fifth, and perhaps the most promising, are policies aimed at institutionalization of education about study drugs. Education could include changes in physician treatment regimen protocols that are formalized by the AMA, including requirements for additional continuing education for pediatricians and family physicians to learn about non-medical treatment options and the potential for diversion of these medications. Potential for diversion also should be instructed to medication users. As mentioned earlier in this review, at least one study has examined the prevalence rates of prescribed college stimulant users being approached to divert their stimulant medication. Of the undergraduate students who were medically prescribed stimulant medication for ADHD, approximately 54% had been approached to divert their medication (e.g. sell, trade or give away) in the past year. Means to protect these students from those that might lure or coerce them into providing their stimulant medication to others are needed. Possibly, college-level prevention programs could be developed to include resistance to offers of study drugs other than those prescribed by a physician. One recommendation that has been made in the New York University Health Center is that those persons prescribed ADHD drugs while in college should keep their drug in a private location, and give reasons for not providing the drugs to others (e.g., to avoid a potential allergic reaction, not enough to share, claim that one has stopped using the drug)

Instruction in good study skills is one way to try to bypass reliance on cramming for exams and associated prescription medication diversion. There are a variety of self-help courses that universities provide to help improve study skills (e.g., at Virginia Polytechnic Institute). These skills involve time management (e.g., scheduling classes and study times, keeping track of tasks to be completed [task lists, charting work tasks on a timeline]), placing a priority on studying (treating it as a full-time job), identifying and removing time wasters, and learning how to concentrate better (e.g., removing distractions from environment, studying in fixed locations, using a timer to increase concentration time, taking scheduled breaks). Cognitive-behavior therapy is popularly suggested for treatment of study drug abuse, but little empirical data exists specifically on its use with these drugs.

## Conclusion

"Study drug" misuse deserves more study. It appears to be concentrated in certain groups for whom programming might be tailored (e.g., males who abide by a fraternity college lifestyle, persons with friends or associates who are prescribed the medication). Abuse occurs when used in rather high doses (orally) or when administered intransally or injected. Monitoring its spread among at risk populations is important. Aggressive marketing of study habit courses is needed. Youth that illegally use these prescription stimulant drugs are relatively likely to use other drugs and suffer from drug abuse. They are also relatively likely to incur serious damage from improper administration of these drugs. Strong warning labels may help, but may be limited as a means of drug control. Much more work is needed on prescription stimulant misuse assessment, reducing access, prevention, cessation, and on identifying the social and economic costs of its misuse.

# Psychoactive Substances Available in Cyberspace Cause Harm

Eduardo Cinosi, Ornella Corazza, Rita Santacroce, Matteo Lupi, Tiziano Acciavatti, Giovanni Martinotti, and Massimo di Giannantonio

Eduardo Cinosi and Rita Santacroce are affiliated with the neuroscience and imaging department at G. d'Annunzio University in Chieti, Italy, and the School of Life and Medical Sciences at the University of Hertfordshire in Hatfield, UK. Ornella Corazza is also affiliated with the neuroscience and imaging department at G. d'Annunzio University, while Matteo Lupi, Tiziano Acciavatti, and Massimo di Giannantonio are affiliated with the School of Life and Medical Sciences at University of Hertfordshire.

The term "new psychoactive substances" (NPS) had been legally defined earlier by the European Union as a new narcotic or psychotropic drug, in pure form or in a preparation, that is, not scheduled under the Single Convention on Narcotic Drugs of 1961 or the Convention on Psychotropic Substances of 1971, but which may pose a public health threat comparable to that posed by substances listed in those conventions (Council of the European Union decision 2005/387/JHA). That legal definition is now widely used and has also been adopted by the European Monitoring Centre for Drugs and Drug Addiction (EMCDDA). The term "new" does not necessarily refer to newly synthetized substances but to a wide range of products that have recently become available on illicit drug market. Many NPS were indeed synthesized and patented decades ago for research purposes, but only recently their chemistry or process of synthesis has been rediscovered or slightly modified to produce effects similar to known illicit substances. In this paper,

"New Drugs on the Internet: The Case of Camfetamine," by Eduardo Cinosi, Ornella Corazza, Rita Santacroce, Matteo Lupi, Tiziano Acciavatti, Giovanni Martinotti, and Massimo di Giannantonio, BioMed Research International, July 16, 2014, https://www. hindawi.com/journals/bmri/2014/419026/.

the authors focus on this specific compound N-methyl-3-phenyl-norbornan-2-amine (Camfetamine), a stimulant drug with effects similar to amphetamine. Precisely, N-methyl-3-phenyl-norbornan-2-amine was developed and patented as an analeptic by Merck, Darmsradt, in 1961. Its synthesis was also described by a group in Smith Kline and French Laboratories when it was prepared as a part of a study to elucidate the stereochemistry of 3-phenyl-norbornan-2-amine; however, it was never commercialized. Indeed, the N-ethyl analogue of 3-phenyl-norbornan-2-amine (Fencamfamine) is better known and has been sold under the trade name Reactivan as a central nervous system (CNS) stimulant and appetite suppressant, also prescribed for reduced performance and for rehabilitation after prolonged and debilitating diseases. Fencamfamine seems also to have been frequently reported as dope substance in sport. While Fencamfamine is listed in the Schedule IV of the UN Convention on Psychotropic Substances, Camfetamine is not listed and appears worldwide mostly unregulated; some exceptions are represented by Portugal, Hungary, and Poland. Recently, the Association of Independent Research Chemical Retailers (AIRCR), an umbrella organization for a number of online vendors, has redeveloped it for use as a recreational drug. According to our online monitoring activity, the first reports about Camfetamine misuse appeared in May 2011. Concomitantly, in 2011 Camfetamine was reported among NPS seizures by official authorities in several countries as United Kingdom, Finland, and Israel. In 2013, Camfetamine was identified in mixtures with methoxetamine, caffeine, taurine, and methiopropamine in Germany. However, very little information is still available in the scientific literature on Camfetamine nature and potential health risks related to its use as a recreational drug.

[...]

## Information on Camfetamine Availability and Consumption

In general, the Internet seems to be an important source to obtain NPS worldwide. The significant informational, promotional, and distributional capacity of the Internet plays an important role in the NPS market and global web-based marketing and distribution distinct from illegal street markets has developed in past years. Our research has identified 12 different websites in which customers can easily buy Camfetamine online. The Internet seems to offer many advantages to NPS suppliers as it provides access to a vast number of potential users and suppliers who do not need large upfront investments and can retain some level of anonymity. It is important to point out that, in many cases, sellers fail to list ingredients hence raising further concerns in terms of the presence of contaminating agents, side effects, or drug interactions of the advertised product. According to our searches, the first online reports on Camfetamine use as recreational drug appeared in May 2011 both in Italy and UK with enthusiastic expectations among users and potential users. Camfetamine is sold as a white or brownish-yellow, clumpy, odourless, and salty powder. The average prices are €11: 250 mg; €20: 500 mg; €38 per gram; €70: 2 g; €160: 5 g. It is most commonly sniffed or taken by oral ingestion (frequent is the "bombing" technique, e.g., wrapping Camfetamine in a cigarette paper and swallowing it, or to melt it in drinks). Other ways of consumption include smoking, intramuscular injection, intravenous, and even rectal administration. Average doses range between 50 and 200 mg. Furthermore, redosing appears to be a common practice and typically involves the intake of more than one dose of 50–100 mg, with the total consumption up to 150–250 mg.

[...]

## Desired Effects and Side Effects

"Smooth" onset has been frequently reported. The effects are described to reach the "high" within an hour and last for 4-5 hours. Unlike other stimulants, many users have reported the need to repeatedly redose this compound in order to get any appreciable stimulant or recreational value. Desired effects include a marked improvement in mental alertness, feeling of clarity, and a stimulant effect followed by a sense of calmness and relaxation. Some experiences report that it also acts as a modest appetite suppressant and improves fatigue. Users report mood changes ranging from no mood enhancement to general pleasant mood or light euphoria at higher doses. On the other hand, users searching for strong euphoric/stimulant effects appear to be critical and disappointed about Camfetamine reporting that it is relatively ineffective and suggesting to choose other stimulants or to use it in combination with other substances.

Side effects manifested up to 24 hours after the intake including anxiety, headache, depressed or disphoric mood, unpleasant body sensations, and severe sleep impairment. However, some users do not report any side effects. About adverse reactions, unlike "classic" stimulants such as cocaine or amphetamine, Camfetamine seems not to be commonly associated with severe physical sympathomimetic effects such as hypertension or respiratory difficulties. Camfetamine is described by most of the users to moderately increase heart/pulse rate, give a light temperature increase, cause slight urinary retention, and dilate pupils. All users report, after insufflation, extremely unpleasant caustic burning sensations to nasal mucous membrane tissue associated with runny nose, squeezing, lacrimation, and corrosive feelings to the throat. Higher doses do seem to increase the stimulant effects of the drug but they also determine an increase in the toxicity. Worrisome data issued in our research are related to intramuscular or intravenous use of Camfetamine that appear to be particularly toxic. It can cause severe local pain in the site of puncture with marked vasoconstriction, painful muscle tension and stiffness, ataxia, blurred vision, muscle weakness, violent incontrollable diffuse tremors, bruxism, and dystonia. For this reason, some users do not recommend IV or IM administration even after complex chemical processes of purification and recrystallization. Within the sample considered in our online monitoring, Camfetamine is commonly taken in conjunction with many other psychoactive substances such as alcohol, cannabis, cocaine, heroin, amphetamine, Metamphetamine, MDMA as well as the less common Methiopropamine (MPA), 5,6-methylenedioxy-2-aminoindane (MDAI), methoxetamine (MXE), N,N-dimethyltryptamine (DMT), α-pyrrolidinopropiophenone (α-PPP), 6-(2-aminopropyl)benzofuran (6-APB), Kanna, Kratom, Dimethocaine, and Prolintane. This polydrug use might be associated with a wide number of unknown side effects/adverse reactions that are potentially lethal. Like for other stimulants, Camfetamine is also used in combination with various medications to self-treat unpleasant effects due to its intake: sedative/hypnotics for agitation and insomnia (Etizolam, Lorazepam, Temazepam, and Clomethiazole), anticonvulsant/myorelaxants for muscle tension and tremors (Pregabalin, Lamotrigine, and Tizanidines), and antiemetic for nausea (Domperidone). Furthermore, many Camfetamine users admit to be under current psychiatric treatment (e.g., with antidepressants, mood stabilizers), without specifying the diagnosis, or under current opioid substitution/analgesic therapy (Methadone, Buprenorphine, Naltrexone, Tramadol, O-Desmethyltramadol, Codeine, Oxycodone, and Fentanyl) and state to mix and misuse also other products (e.g., with Methylphenidate and Modafinil) for recreational purposes.

## Conclusions

The amphetamine-type stimulants class has always been characterized by a large variety of substances. Among these, Camfetamine represents just one of the latest trends within the drug market. Starting from May 2011, N-methyl-3-phenyl-norbornan-2-amine has been redeveloped for use as a recreational drug. To the best of our knowledge, this is the first paper providing both an overview of the current scientific data available on Camfetamine and a critical analysis of the information related to its psychoactive effects, side effects, and use in combination with other drugs.

Camfetamine may act as an indirect dopaminergic agonist in the central nervous system and may have mild-moderate opioid activity too. It produces increased mental alertness, relaxation and, unlike many other stimulants, seems not to be associated with severe physical effects. Only little is known in terms of risks; one could argue about the possible risks associated with ingesting a drug that presents with potential for dependence and the anecdotal report on injecting use. A valid cause for concern issued in our research may be its use in conjunction with other psychoactive substances.

Nowadays, Camfetamine is largely available online and thus "just a click" away from our homes and potentially available to everyone. Moreover, the Internet serves as a repository of information for several groups of people and drug users can obtain information through online forums, chat rooms, and blogs and find out about new products. They can also communicate with other users on their experiences, the effects of the substances, and the recommended sources and avenues of delivery. The apparent possibility to purchase Camfetamine from Websites makes this drug very easily available to vulnerable individuals, including children and adolescents. Vulnerable individuals might be encouraged by a range of widely available online comments/messages/videos related to Camfetamine intake experiences. This may be an issue of concern if one considers that an estimated 61% of young European people aged between 15 and 24 years typically quote the Internet as a potential source of information on drugs. Furthermore, Camfetamine seems to be mostly unregulated and this may facilitate its popularity as well as the users' perception of risks associated with its consumption. The idea that legality can equate with safety still remains well grounded amongst some recreational users. There are no current epidemiological data about Camfetemine use as recreational drug: our research shows that it exsists and mostly in individuals with a history of recreational polydrug misuse. Moreover, the fact that our research was carried out using the Google search engine just in two languages (English and Italian) might underestimate the Camfetamine diffusion.

A possible limitation of our analysis could be given by the fact that publicly available websites, fora, and similar sources were monitored. One could wonder about many limitations of carrying out a risk of misuse assessment of a drug while taking into account the online comments. First, it may be inappropriate to trust information obtained from the Internet without independent verification. Second, the present findings do rely on what is reported by users and we did not have any possibility here to ascertain if the substance the online alleged drug users were taking was indeed N-methyl-3-phenyl-norbornan-2-amine. Third, Camfetamine effects/adverse reactions are described in our qualitative analysis by a population of polyabusers as having most probably a high tolerance to many substances, and some of them declare even to be drug addicted or under current psychiatric treatment. Globally, Camfetamine users considered in our analysis, added together, are also intaking alcohol, cannabis, cocaine, heroin, amphetamine and synthetic amphetamine derivatives, Piperazine-based derivatives, Mephedrone, Pipradrol and derivatives, aminoindane analogues, Ketamine and derivatives, synthetic cannabinoid receptor agonists, Tryptamines, Benzofurans and Benzodifurans, natural product (Fungal and Herbal) novel psychoactive substances, Benzodiazepines, Barbiturates, anticonvulsant, antidepressants, and opioid substitution/analgesic therapies. Such a phenomenon constitutes a serious public health challenge: pharmacological, toxicological, and psychopathological effects due to interactions among all these substances may be unpredictable and fatal in vulnerable individuals. Moreover, such a chronic polydrug intake may lead to neurobiochemical CNS alteration that might make these polyabusers extremely difficult to be pharmacologically treated even by expert mental health professionals. On the other hand, online reports about the experience with Camfetamine seem genuine and many users illustrate their detailed experiences with Camfetamine as proper experiments (see Re: Camfetamine). Thus, in the absence of relevant peer-reviewed data, the online monitoring seems to be indeed the only method to obtain preliminary information about new and emergent phenomena. One could conclude that a constant web-monitoring activity with respect to drug-related issues is necessary to better understand the level of the diffusion of novel psychoactive substances such as Camfetamine. It is here suggested that better international collaboration levels may be needed to tackle the novel and fast growing phenomenon of novel psychoactive drugs availability from the web. Furthermore, it is here highlighted that more large-scale studies need to be carried out to confirm and better describe the extent as well as the risks of Camfetamine use in the European Union and elsewhere. Again, health and other professionals should be rapidly informed about this and other new and alerting trends of misuse. In this context, we suggest that the use of technological tools could be successfully incorporated in specific prevention programmes targeted at both health professionals and young people looking for reliable information about novel psychoactive substances.

# Organizations to Contact

*The editors have compiled the following list of organizations concerned with the issues debated in this book. The descriptions are derived from materials provided by the organizations. All have publications or information available for interested readers. This list was compiled on the date of publication of the present volume; the information provided here may change. Be aware that many organizations take several weeks or longer to respond to inquiries, so allow as much time as possible.*

**BioMed Central (BMC)**
One New York Plaza
Suite 4600
New York, NY 10004-1562
phone: (800) 777-4643
website: www.biomedcentral.com

A pioneer in open-access publishing, BMC manages a portfolio of high-quality, peer-reviewed databases and periodicals to advance knowledge and understanding of the biomedical sciences.

**Center for Drug Evaluation and Research**
White Oak Building 51
6th Floor
10903 New Hampshire Avenue
Silver Spring, MD 20993
phone: (310) 796-5400
email: CDERCENTERDIRECTOR@fda.hhs.gov
website: www.fda.gov/about-fda/center-drug-evaluation-and-research/center-drug-evaluation-and-research

The Center for Drug Evaluation and Research is a part of the FDA that focuses on ensuring that safe and effective drugs are available to improve the health of consumers. They ensure health benefits outweigh risks and that new medical therapies work correctly.

**The Center for Economic and Policy Research (CEPR)**
1611 Connecticut Avenue NW
Suite 400
Washington, DC 20009
phone: (202) 293-5380
website: www.cepr.net

The CEPR promotes democratic debate on the most important economic and social issues that affect people's lives. CEPR is committed to presenting issues in an accurate and understandable manner, enabling the public to be better prepared to choose among policy options.

**National Academy of Science**
505 Fifth Street NW
Washington, DC 20001
phone: (202) 334-2000
website: www.nasonline.org

The National Academy of Science is a private, nonprofit society charged with providing independent and objective advice to the nation on matters relating to science and technology.

**National Attorneys General Training and Research Institute (NAAGTRI)**
1850 M Street NW
12th Floor
Washington, DC 20036
phone: (202) 326-6000
email: lthrash@naag.org
website: www.naag.org

The mission of the NAAGTRI is to provide high-quality, nonpartisan, and innovative training, research, and other developmental resources to support state attorneys general.

**National Institute on Drug Abuse**
Office of Science Policy and Communications
Public Information and Liaison Branch
6001 Executive Boulevard
Room 5213, MSC 9561
Bethesda, MD 20892
phone: (301) 443-1124
website: www.drugabuse.gov

The National Institute on Drug Abuse is dedicated to advancing science on the causes and consequences of drug use and addiction, and applying that knowledge to improve individual and public health.

**Pew Research Center**
1615 L Street NW
Suite 800
Washington, DC 20036
phone: (202) 419-4300
email: info@pewresearch.org
website: www.pewresearch.org

The Pew Research Center is a nonpartisan fact tank that informs the public about issues, attributes, and trends shaping America and the world. The center conducts public opinion polling, demographic research, content analysis, and other data-driven social science research.

**Pharmaceutical Research and Manufacturers of America (PRMA)**
950 F Street NW
Suite 300
Washington, DC 20004
phone: (202) 835-3400
website: www.phrma.org

PRMA conducts effective advocacy for public policies that encourage the discovery of important new medicines for patients by biopharmaceutical research companies.

### The Reason Foundation
1747 Connecticut Avenue NW
Washington, DC 20009
phone: (202) 986-0916
website: www.reason.org

The Reason Foundation aims to advance a free society by developing, applying, and promoting libertarian principles including individual liberty, free markets, and the rule of law.

### Social Justice Foundation
801 Garden Street
Suite 101
Santa Barbara, CA 93101
phone: (805) 899-8620
email: infor@tsjf.org
website: www.thesocialjusticefoundation.org

The Social Justice Foundation is a public benefit organization that strives to not just inform, but also promote meaningful public dialogue by widely disseminating scientific research in the areas of economic, educational, environmental, and social justice.

# Bibliography

## Books

Claire D. Clark. *The Recovery Revolution: The Battle Over Addiction Treatment in the United States*. New York, NY: Columbia University Press, 2017.

Phillip J. Cook. *Paying the Tab: The Costs and Benefits of Alcohol Control*. Princeton, NJ: Princeton University Press, 2016.

Steve Elliott. *The Little Black Book of Marijuana: The Essential Guide to the World of Cannabis, 3rd Edition*. White Plains, NY: Peter Pauper Press, 2012.

Peter Hecht. *Weed Land: Inside America's Marijuana Epicenter and How Pot Went Legit*. Berkeley, CA: University of California Press, 2014.

Mark A. R. Kleiman, Jonathan P. Caulkins, and Angela Hawken. *Drugs and Drug Policy: What Everyone Needs to Know*. Oxford, UK: Oxford University Press, 2011.

Michael Pollan. *How to Change Your Mind: What the Science of Psychedelics Teaches us About Consciousness, Dying, Addiction, Depression and Transcendence*. New York, NY: Penguin Press, 2018.

Ben Sessa. *The Psychedelic Renaissance, 2nd Edition*. London, UK: Muswell Hill Press, 2017.

William O. Walker III. *Drug Control Policy: Essays in Historical and Comparative Perspective, 3rd Edition*. University Park, PA: Pennsylvania State University Press, 1992.

## Periodicals and Internet Sources

Rachel Barclay, "4 Illegal Drugs That Might Be Medicines," *Healthline Media*, November 30, 2013. https://www.

healthline.com/health-news/mental-four-illegal-drugs-with-medicinal-qualities-113013#1.

Jonathan P. Caulkins, Anna Kasunic, Mark Kleiman, and Michael A.C. Lee, "Understanding Drug Legalization," *International Public Health Journal*, July 1, 2014. https://www.questia.com/library/journal/1P3-3499280331/understanding-drug-legalization.

Loren DeVito, "When Legal Drugs Harm and Illegal Drugs Help," *Scientific American*, December 1, 2017. https://blogs.scientificamerican.com/observations/when-legal-drugs-harm-and-illegal-drugs-help/?redirect=1.

Marc Lallanilla, "6 Party Drugs That Have Health Benefits," *LiveScience,* November 18, 2013. https://www.livescience.com/41277-health-benefits-illegal-drugs.html.

Celia J. A. Morgan, Louise A. Noronha, Mark Muetzelfeldt, Amanda Fielding, and H. Valerie Curran, "Harms and Benefits Associated with Psychoactive Drugs: Findings of an International Survey of Active Drug Users," *Journal of Psychopharmacology*, June 2013. https://www.ncbi.nlm.nih.gov/pmc/articles/PMC4107777/.

David Nutt, "Beyond Cannabis: Why We Should Look at Legalising Other Drugs for Medical Use to Benefit Patients," *Pharmaceutical Journal,* October 24, 2018. https://www.pharmaceutical-journal.com/opinion/comment/beyond-cannabis-why-we-should-look-at-legalising-other-illegal-drugs-for-medical-use-to-benefit-patients/20205613.article?firstPass=false.

Shami Sivasubramanian, "7 Illegal Drugs That Could Be Used in Medicine," SBS, May 20, 2016. https://www.sbs.com.au/topics/science/humans/article/2016/05/20/7-illegal-drugs-could-be-used-medicine.

# Index